Thinking C++
Part I

Dr. Randy Kaplan

A Publication of the Programming Institute
May 2017

Table of Contents

Forward

Another book about C++ programming. Do we really need another book about C++ programming? Aren't there enough books about C++ programming? Well as a long time programmer, I personally think there can never be enough books about C++ programming. In fact, I believe our poor performance in teaching novices how to program supports this notion. We have lots of books but how is it that we fail so miserably when we try to teach programming?

One problem is that the institutions that teach programming have not changed their basic teaching approach in years. They certainly have not paid much attention to the data about teaching programming and in not paying attention they have missed some of the problems induced by the way we teach people to program. So, yes, one more book about programming.

Another important aspect of the way that we program is that most of the people teaching others to program have not done a substantial amount of programming themselves.* This means they are teaching with a deficit before they even begin to teach programming. It cannot be assumed that a person teaching you to program actually KNOWS how to program and has done any substantial amount of programming. The author, for example, has over 40 years of programming experience. Few teachers, teaching programming in the university have anywhere near that much experience.†

Most of us "old heads" who learned to program in the day when computers were not so ubiquitous had to take a different approach to programming a computer. We had to somehow become the computer. We had to imagine that we were following the instruction in a computer program and that we could see what was happening in the program. That may sound as if it would be impossible; to imagine what a program does as it is running in this seemingly ultra-complex machine. The truth is that the complexity of the machine has nothing to do with learning to program. Because we are human beings and because WE invented programming languages so we could write programs we should be able to follow the instructions in a program in order to understand what the computer is doing. Unfortunately, this particular bit is missing from most classes in programming and

---

* If the reader will be teaching programming it is suggested that they take a look at and obtain a copy of "Teaching Programing," a new book by this author scheduled to be released in 2017.

† Although some might want to convince you of their experience through their braggadocio.

students have to suffer along in painful silence while they are writing, re-writing, and re-re-writing programs until they run. After a fashion they may learn what the program is actually doing but typically by the end of a CS1 type course they have little understanding of what they are doing, and CS2 turns into a disaster for them.

The approach I espouse in this book is quite different from other books but it is not a new approach as far as programming goes. After watching students struggle with their programs again and again and after thinking about what is missing from their education it dawned on me that what was missing was the very thing that we all have to do when we learned something new. We had to understand what was happening in order to understand how to do it. That makes a lot of sense doesn't it? We had to understand it first before we did it. A simple example of this in practice is the table saw.

Let a person approach a table saw and ask them to cut a piece of wood in a certain way without any prior instruction and you are taking a huge risk. Chances are without that instruction they will lose a finger or two in the process. Now I know there are some teachers that believe that losing a finger or two WILL result in a lesson, but there are less painful ways to learn and one would definitely question the methods of these teachers who espouse the table saw approach to programming.

I would never touch a computer unless I knew what it was doing. In fact my first experiences with a computer were so horrendous that I often thought I could never be a programmer. It was just impossible to write instructions that the damn thing would understand. Over the years though I learned to understand computers in terms of how they understood my instructions and this made all the difference.

The premise of this book is that you don't have to have a computer in order to learn to program one. In case you are interested you cannot learn to be a programmer in an hour or in a day. That just isn't possible. Those students brought up on such notions are in for a big surprise when they arrive to their first programming classes. The approach today is just part of that notion that we must give students immediate gratification and it doesn't matter that they understand what they are doing. Of course we in higher education receive these students and we must re-introduce the reality of programming to them.

So for all of you who have picked up this book and do plan to read it, there are two requests that I ask you to agree to before reading this book. First, that you pay attention to the details. There is an old saying that the "devil is in the details," and in programming that saying was never so true. You must attend to the details in order to become a programmer. There is no getting away from this. Second is that as you are reading this book, at no time will you employ a computer to do anything in this book. You will use your mind to do all of the work. After all it is still the case that the mind in the most powerful computer in existence today. It can handle deciphering code and follow the instructions. It may not be as fast as a computer, but it is certainly as competent as any computer. If you agree to these two things, then proceed. And if not, please, return this book, and purchase one of the 100's of other "How to program in C++" books. You will be doing yourself a favor and also making less bother for me.

But will I be able to learn to program a computer?

(You may completely ignore the follow section of this book as it may be somewhat discouraging.)

There is a trend today that would indicate that ANYONE can learn to program a computer. The trend is indicated by such things as the "learn-to-program-in-a-day" efforts that have been going on for the past couple of years. To me, it is unfortunate that these efforts have been going on because in the end they are not proven. There is no data that proves the success of these programs. In my days as a software engineer, I have learned the following about wanting to learn to program. They can roughly be divided in several classes which include:

- The Naturals (best or highest level)
- The Naturals –
- The Workers
- The Workers –
- The Shouldn't Be's (lowest level)

For the most part these categories are self explanatory. They do not say anything about whether a Worker- could in fact move up a level to a Worker or down a level to a Shouldn't Be. The only purpose these serve is to delineate the "pre-skill" levels of people who are learning to program. With this information it may give you some insight into whether or not your student or student would turn out to be a viable or in-viable programmer. For those of you using this book as a vehicle for teaching programming, you can use the above categories to gain some idea of the challenge you face. For those of you using this book as a vehicle for learning C++ you will be able to understand something about your frustration level as you proceed.

Keep in mind, these categorizations are only meant as a "help" from my own experience and in fact may not be valid or apply at all. I take no responsibility for any outcome that comes of paying attention to these classifications.

Chapter 1 Introduction A Lost Art Lately Discovered

There has been a discovery lately that we are going to need many more people trained to program computers than we currently have trained to program computers. It is interesting that President Clinton and President Obama has finally made this a national priority because this situation has been around for at least 10 years if not longer. Look back at the Bureau of Labor Statistics forecasts on the number of programmers we will need and you will be astounded by the projected numbers. Why didn't someone notice this earlier. One of the reasons is that we are a nation of reactionaries. If there is a crisis we react to it. But enough about this. Let's get back to the subject at hand.

Our approach to increasing the number of kids interested in computers as a career is to get them to code for an hour or a day. This is sort of a funny way to get kids interested because a day may work for some kids, but as those of us in the field know, programming can be extremely challenging and frustrating. This has also been written about by researchers over the past 10 years, and there has been no remedy for the problem. There are so many cognitive skills involved with programming that to learn all of them at once is almost an impossible task. Only the students it seems who have innate skills for programming will catch on and usually this will happen very quickly. What compounds this problem is that today a person has access to amazing technology (game playing computers, cellular telephones) which are "so simple" to use. This leads to the assumption that it must not be too difficult to develop the programs these devices run on. But the truth is that it is far from simple and in any first year/first term programming course many students are "turned off" by programming because of this not to mention things fall out of their course. It is "not for them." This is fine because we don't want just anyone in the field, but how many perspective students are we losing who might in fact turn out to be talented programmers? I wonder if anyone has done any research in this area. Another problem is that we have no predictive model for success to be a programmer.

The requirement that a language is not forgiving is something most people have never encountered and therefore results in many errors in the beginning. We are so used to our brains being forgiving and able to figure out things that we assume that everything we encounter is going to work like this. Unfortunately, when it comes to computers this is not the case. Computers, as I've said, are not forgiving and expect you to follow the rules rigidly. That is why an hour of coding or a day of coding will not be sufficient to "learn to program." In fact, usually, learning to program in one of these day of coding events amounts to nothing more than dragging and dropping shapes that do certain things. Once you know what a shape does you can create simple programs. An actual programming language has no shapes to drag. It uses words, sentences, and paragraphs to assemble a program. That's the basics of how we will learn a programming language. We will learn it as we are learning any other human language and in the process we will not use a computer as the proof we are understanding the programming language correctly. We will learn what sentences mean and be able to construct paragraphs in the language. Finally, we will learn what essays mean in a programming language and at that point we are ready to mentally run our programs – but not until that time will we be writing our own programs. Before that time, we will not be using a computer to verify the programs we write.

Part of the complexity about learning to program is that programming involves many subtasks – perhaps too many subtasks. When we teach programming we teach all of the subtasks at one time. We teach students how to use the environments to write and run programs, we teach them a new language, and we teach them how to read and write in this new language. Even in foreign language classes the cognitive challenges are broken down into separate skills and this is only a single skill. There is no problem solving, and there is no "environment" to learn. Nevertheless, we teach programming as if it is like any other subject and we are not very successful doing it. There have been many papers written about this very topic (see commentary https://andy.wordpress.com/2012/05/30/programming-is-not-algebra/).

The "Lost Art" referred to at the beginning of this chapter is taking programming and breaking it into its subtasks and teach those subtasks separately. If I wish to teach you how to program a computer, I want to teach you the language and how to speak it, then how to problem solve with it, then how to give the computer the program you are writing, and then teach you how to run and test the programs that you write. The novelty in the approach taken by this book is that you won't need a computer to learn to program which is an assumption underlying this book.

Those of us who began to program when computers came on the scene learned to do it without any computer. Why? Because computers were large and expensive machines, and access to them for learning was limited. Someone would have to spend millions of dollars for a single computer, so it just wasn't possible to sit in front of a computer display and write. We had to do our programming **by thinking about what we were doing first, and then writing the program in a programming language, and then thinking about whether the program would run successfully**.

So this book teaches you how to program by putting you in the shoes of a computer. You have to think like a computer and analyze your programs just as the computer would analyze your program. You will also have to run your program without a computer. You will be the computer that runs your program. In this book you will learn how the computer does what it does so that you can do what the computer does. This is a great departure from how computer programming is taught today. At first you might think, that's ridiculous. Well that is okay, you can think that. But don't discount it before you give it a try. You'd be surprised about how once you understand what the computer is doing how much easier the task of computing becomes. With that said, let's jump into that pool and start swimming.

From web page: http://www-03.ibm.com/ibm/history/ibm100/us/en/icons/system360/

Chapter 2 Learning a Programming Language is like Learning Any Other Language

Have you ever learned another language in school? Most of us will have done that and perhaps you can remember how the language was taught. You started at the beginning of the language. The beginning was either words in the language or even the alphabet of the language. The purpose of the latter, alphabet first, is to teach you how to pronounce the letters of the language. There is no pronunciation to learn in a programming language. So we can jump right into the words of the language following the pattern used when we teach a foreign natural language*.

In this book you will learn the words in the language. One important difference is that the words must be spelled exactly as you are shown. There can be no deviation. If a letter is shown as a capital letter it must be capitalized. If the letter is a lower case letter, it must be written in lower case. When there is an option, you will be told. Writing words in the language is the first step to learning a programming language.

Along with writing the words, comes learning what the words mean. When you encounter the word d-o-g for the first time when you are young and learning English you may not know what the 3 letters stand for (although today most kids have heard this word at an early age). Let's assume though you've never seen the letters and once you pronounce the word you need to know what the word refers to. You need to know the definition of the word. It is exactly the same when learning a programming language. We will be showing you words in the new language and telling you what they mean. In programming terms, the meaning of a word is defined by what purpose the word serves.

* The term natural is used to denote a language that is spoken by human beings.

Once we cover some of the words of the language we will then explain how to make sentences in the language – meaning how to assemble the words into meaningful sequences of words. Like learning any other language it is critical to learn how to write meaningful sentences in the language. This is especially true in the case of a programming language where it is extremely easy to write sentences that have no meaning if you violate the rules of writing a program in programming language sentences. This is very different than writing in English. Whereas a human's brain can compensate for inaccuracies in language, a computer has no such ability. It cannot compensate and it takes anything and everything you write literally, so if you spell something incorrectly it will try to figure out what it means and if it can't it will throw the sentence out if it is a bad one. **Learning to write a correct sentence in a programming language is one of the most important skills you can learn first when learning to write a program for a computer.** Secondarily you must also understand what the sentence you write means.

Once you can compose sentences in the language we will show you how to create paragraphs in the programming language. That's right, just as a natural language has paragraphs, so too does a computer language have paragraphs. And like a programming language's sentences, the paragraphs are assembled with very specific rules. If a paragraph is assembled that violates the rules of assembling a paragraph in a programming language the computer will not understand the paragraph and tell you so.

After being able to write paragraphs correctly, paragraphs are assembled into compositions or even larger works (essays, books, etc.). These parts of learning a programming language are actually creating the programs which make the computer carry out specific tasks. Like all other elements of a programming language, the rules for assembling essays, for example, are very specific and must not be violated.

Onward … let's start to learn the vocabulary of the programming language. Remember the words allow you to construct sentences in the language. It is not until you understand what the words are for (what they represent) that you will understand how to create sentences. In the beginning of Thinking C++ we will focus on the punctuation and vocabulary of the C++ language.

Chapter 3
Vocabulary of C++

So as I promised, the first part of learning a language is learning the vocabulary of the language, how the words are used, and what they mean. As these words will be a core aspect of the language C++ it is very important to pay attention to what they are, how they are written, where they can be used, etc., etc. Like any other language, using a word incorrectly can change the meaning of a sentence, so although you may not think this is an important part of learning the C++ language I assure you it is and it will pay off for you when you begin writing programs in C++.

In addition to words I will also identify punctuation in the language. It always seemed to me that the rules for punctuation in English were somewhat ambiguous – at least the teachers that I had did not take too much time to make explicitly clear where a particular punctuation mark was used. There was an implicit expectation that we somehow understood what the rules were and therefore should already know them. In programming, punctuation is **VERY** important and the rules for using punctuation are defined clearly by the rules of the language. So as I proceed in describing the punctuation, keep in mind where and how the punctuation symbols are used. An error in use will cause the compiler (the program that transforms your program into machine understandable language) to produce an error when processing your program. Errors in punctuation are always difficult to find because they are so small – both literally and figuratively.

Punctuation in C++

The table below lists the punctuation in C++ you must understand if you are going to write programs in C++. In addition to the actual symbol used for a particular punctuation, we also describe what purpose the punctuation serves when it issued.

Punctuation Symbol	Punctuation Description
;	Semi-colon. Primarily used to indicate the end of a sentence in the C++ programming language. There are exceptions to this use which will be described. A semi-colon is like the period (.) in English that is typically used to end a sentence.
,	A comma is a separator character. Typically when you are writing a list of things, each item in that list will be separated from the next item with a comma as in the list a,b,c,d,e,f
{ } (Left and Right brace)	These symbols, the left and right brace are always used in a pair. The left brace, sometimes called the opening brace, is never without its other half, the right brace, or closing brace. It is typically the case that the left brace is some lines away from its companion right brace. These braces are used to delineate what amounts to paragraphs in the C++ language. Groups of individual sentences are enclosed in braces to create paragraphs in the C++ language.
"…"	The double quote (the quote that is made from two apostrophes). These come in pairs and typically will enclose some other characters. The ellipsis (…) represents what the quotes enclose. Typically, the pair of double quotes enclose a sequence of characters. When you enclose characters in quotes the characters are taken literally – that is to say they are not transformed in any way by the compiler‡. Never forget to include the closing double quote at the end of the sequence of characters that begin with a quotation mark. If you do forget the closing quote this will lead to a

‡ A compiler is a specialized computer program. This means that since it consists of a series of instructions that the computer can understand, it consists of 1's and 0's just like any other computer data. The instructions that make up a compiler transform programs into 1's and 0's understood by a computer as a computer program. Whenever the term compiler is mentioned we are talking about this specialized computer program.

	disaster because the remaining characters that make up your program will be rendered meaningless when forgetting the second quotation mark. The program excerpt show below demonstrates how a compiler will deal with a missing quotation mark.
	
	`Randys-MacBook-Air:~ rkaplan$ g++ HelloWorld.cpp`
	`HelloWorld.cpp:6:11: warning: missing terminating '"' character [-Winvalid-pp-token]`
	`cout << "Hello World\n;`
	`^`
	
	`HelloWorld.cpp:6:11: error: expected expression`
	`1 warning and 1 error generated.`

[ ]
(Left and right bracket)
	The left and right bracket is used to identify something called an index. The left and right bracket are always in pairs. The opening bracket must have a closing bracket. Note that the left and right brackets and the left and right braces cannot be used interchangeably. They have different meanings and are used in different places in the sentences you will be writing.
	
	Example:
	
	Code:
	
	`#include <iostream>`
	`using namespace std;`
	
	`int golf()`
	`{`
	`int anArray [10};`
	`cout << "Hello World\n;`
	`return 0;`
	`}`
	
	Result:

```
HelloWorld.cpp:6:18: error: expected ']'
  int anArray [10};
                 ^

HelloWorld.cpp:6:15: note: to match this '['
  int anArray [10};
              ^

HelloWorld.cpp:6:18: error: expected ';' at end of declaration
  int anArray [10};
                 ^
                 ;

HelloWorld.cpp:7:3: error: unknown type name 'cout'
  cout << "Hello World\n;
  ^

HelloWorld.cpp:7:8: error: expected unqualified-id
  cout << "Hello World\n;
       ^

HelloWorld.cpp:7:11: warning: missing terminating '"' character
      [-Winvalid-pp-token]
  cout << "Hello World\n;
          ^

HelloWorld.cpp:9:1: error: extraneous closing brace ('}')
}
^
```

( )
(Left and right parenthesis)

The left and right parenthesis are used to enclose parts of an expression (as in algebraic expression or expression of arithmetic). The left and right parenthesis are always paired. A left parenthesis is never used without its other half, the right parenthesis. Leaving out a left or right parenthesis of a pair will cause an error in your program. Left and right parenthesis are also used to enclose lists as you will see.

Example 1: Mixed Delimiters

Code:

```
include <iostream>
using namespace std;

int  golf()
[
  cout << "Hello World\n;
  int a = {3 + 4];

  return 0;
}
```

Result:

<table>
<tr><td></td><td><pre>HelloWorld.cpp:6:11: warning: missing terminating '"' ch
      [-Winvalid-pp-token]
  cout << "Hello World\n;
          ^

HelloWorld.cpp:6:11: error: expected expression
HelloWorld.cpp:10:2: error: expected '}'
}
 ^

HelloWorld.cpp:5:1: note: to match this '{'
{
^

1 warning and 2 errors generated.</pre></td></tr>
<tr><td>NOTE:</td><td>When you are writing programs it is ALWAYS a good idea when writing paired punctuation symbols like the left and right parenthesis to write both characters of the pair of symbols. This can be a bit tricky as you may not know what you are going to place inside the pair of symbols. The point is that by beginning with the pair of symbols, you will never forget one of the pair. To take care of the problem of not knowing what may go into the symbols, simply leave some space between them when you write them so you have room for what will be written in them.

Examples:
(<br>)
[
]
{
}</td></tr>
<tr><td>'c'
'\"'</td><td>The single apostrophe also always comes in pairs to denote the beginning of a special sequence and the end of a special sequence. This single apostrophe pair typically contains a single character except when the character is an "escaped" character in which case the pair can contain two characters, the first of which is a backslash, and the second of which is a character. When, for example, wanting to display a quotation mark as a quotation character, it must be preceded by a backslash character, followed by the character """, followed by the closing single apostrophe.</td></tr>
<tr><td>:</td><td>The colon is used as a special purpose punctuation character. It appears in certain sentences to separate certain words from one</td></tr>
</table>

	another. Its use is specific to its purpose therefore we will be describing the colon in the context in which it is used.

As we describe the C++ language, we will be describing when and how these punctuation characters are used in your sentences. For the time being you should be aware that there are certain characters (defined in the table above) used for punctuation.

On to the Vocabulary of C++

A C++ World Cloud[§]

Now that we've covered the punctuation characters we can begin to cover the vocabulary. Just as in any spoken language the vocabulary of C++ consists of words that have specific meanings. When first seeing a word it is often difficult to understand the word and how it is used in context. Said differently, how can the word be combined with other words in order to make sense in sentences you write in the language. The reason that we have chosen to break the language up in the way that we have is that this is the very way that we learn words when we learn a language. We are first exposed to the word and given its meaning and then we are shown how the word is used in a sentence. In a programming language the sentences that are made from words are very specific. You cannot deviate from the sentence in which the words are used. In a programming language this defines

[§] A word cloud is a representation of the words used in written material or even a computer program. The words are extracted from a sample of words having t do with the topic at hand (in this case C++) and the number of times a word appears in the sample is counted. The more occurrences of a word causes the word to be displayed larger and closer to the center of the cloud. Words that are used less frequently are smaller and move further away from the center of the word cloud.

specific sentence types. Just as punctuation is used in very special ways and the rules of punctuation cannot be violated, the same can be said of words in the C++ language. The rules that govern how words are used are very specific and deviation from these rules will result in compiler errors**. So if you don't wish to receive compiler errors, pay attention to the rules for using words of the C++ vocabulary.

For a moment, let's consider the English language. There are times when a sentence can begin with a noun or a pronoun. It would be fine to write sentences like,

"Jerry went to the park."
"The automobile drove to the mall."

whereas it would not be okay to construct a sentence like,
"rat chased the dog."*††

The sentence doesn't sound right and usually when this is the case we could assume that there is something wrong with the sentence. The same is true for words in a programming language. Incorrect use of words will make the sentence "sound wrong" in C++ sentences. When you first learn to program in C++ any C++ sentence that you write may seem like gibberish. As you begin to learn and write C++ sentences you will get used to recognizing when C++ sentences sound wrong.

In C++ the words that can be used in sentences are generally called keywords. There are quite a few keywords and of course they all have different purposes when used in C++ sentences. When you learn a language for the very first time, the sentences that you are taught are very simple ones. Naturally, the very simple sentences use a limited number of words that you will learn. Consider if you will that the words we will identify are for the simpler sentences that will follow. Later, as you progress in your learning of the C++ language the sentences will become more complex and necessarily use more of the vocabulary that can be used in the language. The set of words that will be identified are those that will be used in the simpler sentences of C++. Keep that in mind the complete set of keywords is larger than what will be presented here.

** A compiler error is caused when (a) a vocabulary word is spelled incorrectly, or it is used incorrectly. A sentence is incorrectly formed or when a paragraph is improperly specified.

†† In English, when we write an incorrect sentence it is usually marked with as asterisk.

Beginning Vocabulary in the C++ Programming Language

Word	Brief Explanation/Description
break	used to change the behavior of a loop
case	used to specify an option in a switch statement
continue	used to change the behavior of a loop
default	the very last thing to do in a switch statement
do	signifies the start of a loop
else	the other part of an if statement
for	signifies the start of a counting loop
if	signifies the beginning of a conditional statement
import	specifies a library header file should be included
namespace	specifies the list of symbols to be recognized by the compiler
return	specifies that a function is finished its work
switch	Begins a multi-condition conditional statement
using	used in conjunction with the word namespace as in using a namespace
while	signifies the start of a loop

Comment: These words are to be written EXACTLY as shown. In other words, as lower case words. Writing them with any upper case character will cause the compiler to misunderstand the word and display an error.

Side Note: Everything written for a computer to understand can be one of two types of things – either program instructions or data – that is all. The program instructions that process a program (a kind of data) is called a compiler. The compiler translates the program instructions you write into instructions the computer understands.

This set of words is a basic set of words that can be used to start a sentence in the C++ language. There are some other sentential elements (parts of a sentence in C++) that can also be used to start a sentence in the C++ language and they will be described later. For now let's assume this is the basic set of words you are to use to begin sentences in the C++ language.

Some of these words make up a complete sentence. For example:

```
break;
continue;
return;
```

These are examples of complete sentences in the C++ language. If you were to write these, you would be writing a correct sentence in the C++ language. Other words require additional language parts (sentential elements) to create complete sentences. The following words are those that require these additional sentential elements as indicated by the ellipsis (...) .

```
do ... ;
else ...;
for ...;
if ...;
if ... ; else ...;
import ...;
using namespace ...;
return ...;
switch ... case ... default;
while ...;
```

These words constitute a basic set of words the C++ language. If you want to write a sentence in the C++ language you can safely use one of these words as a starting word of the sentence. Of course some of those words will only constitute complete correct sentences when additional parts of the language are added. If a sentence begins otherwise (with some other word) unless described, the compiler will produce an error.

Consider these words the beginning of your C++ vocabulary. You could walk around saying words like break, continue, return and your sentence fragments would be correct.

As sentences in English contain other kinds of words, which do not usually appear at the beginning of a sentence, so too does C++ have words that function in this capacity. Some, like the words that can begin sentences, are in fact single words, while others are more complex constructions based on more primitive parts of the C++ language. Think about the prepositional phrase of a sentence. A prepositional phrase begins with a preposition. A preposition is a word like,

into
of
on
off
at

A prepositional phrase does not end at the preposition. It must have another part to be complete. Adding a noun phrase to the preposition is one way to complete the prepositional phrase. A noun phrase can be a noun (person, place, or thing), or an article (the, a, an) and a noun. Examples of prepositional phrases would include:

into the abyss
of the light
after the fact
on the table
at the races

So we can build up sentences with other sentential elements to make larger fragments that can play a part in a properly written sentence. Here is where the English language begins to differ from programming languages. The sentential elements in C++ are more mathematical (having to do with their use in mathematics) in nature then linguistic (having to do with their use in language). Still they serve the same purpose, namely to build a correct sentence in the programming language.

One of the most common C++ sentential elements is called an expression. An expression is made up of still other sentential elements just as a prepositional phrase is made up of other English elements.

Expressions are such an important kind of sentence element that they get their very own chapter !!

Chapter 4
C++ Expressions

An expression as the name implies, is a specification of a calculation.

The computer can produce many different kinds of values as results and this ability of the computer is what gives the computer its extraordinary power. It is also what gives a programming language its ability to express complex and useful "thoughts."

An expression produces a result. A result of an expression has a value. In programming we say the numbers like 1, 2, 9, 78, 649, and LOLY are values. Each of these values has another characteristic associated with them.

6 Key Parts of an Expression

In any expression there six elements that are important understand, remember, know, etc. They are:

1. Types
2. Constants
3. Variables
4. Operators
5. Punctuation
6. Evaluation

1. Types

As I've said several times, computers must have everything explained to them in order for them to carry out their work correctly. Things that we take for granted cannot be assumed to be known or understood by the computer.

One of these concepts that must be specified for the computer is named type. When we first learned arithmetic, and then math, algebra, and algebra 2 the concept of type was introduced but not as precisely as it should have been. As you know, a value is usually associated with a number of some sort. We are used to seeing values as a part of a calculation.

$$72 + 14 = 86$$

This calculation has three values: 72, 14, and 86. We learned that there can be other kinds of values like real numbers 32.6, -0.07, and 3.14 as examples. Within the real definition of numbers there are types of numbers we call rational and others that we call irrational. Both rational and irrational numbers have whole portions (like integers) and a decimal portion. The decimal portion of a rational number is fixed – it has a definite ending, for example the rational real numbers 32.6, 4.9321, and .073 are rational real numbers.

An irrational number has no definite ending digit. For example when you divide 10 by 3 you get 3.3333333333… and so on.

The point of describing these 3 kinds of numbers, integer, rational and irrational is to define the meaning of type. Type is a description of the characteristics of a group of numbers. The group of characteristics is given a name and the name designates the type of the number. In other words, a type is a list of characteristics of a certain group of numbers. Each type has a unique name. In order to store a type of number in memory and carry out arithmetic operations with it the type of number must be known in order for a value of the type to be stored correctly and operations to be carried out correctly.

2. Constants

Think back to the very first time you practiced arithmetic. You probably learned how to compute

2+2
1+4
3+6
7x9
etc.

Remember those? These are among the simplest expressions that you will encounter. They demonstrate a few of the "rules" of expressions. There are many such rules.

Rule 1: An expression has operands (2, 1, 4, 3, 6, 7, 9)
Rule 2: An expression has at least one operator (+, x)

Rule 3: An expression is computable (you can determine the meaning of the expression by doing what the expression says). This determination of meaning is called **EVALUATION** (6 in our list).

The **EVALUATIONS** of the previous expressions are:

4
5
9
63

The operands (the thing the operation works on) in this case are constants. They never change and will always be the values that are written. In C++ there are several different types of constants. For example, the constants above are called INTEGERS. An integer is a designation of a value type. They are whole numbers with no decimal point. They designate numbers without any smaller parts. A second kind of constant is called a real or floating point number. Examples of these include:

4.31
3.1
55.796
63.0

You might look at the last example and say, hey isn't that a whole number, an integer? Well although it looks like one there is a big difference between 63 and 63.0. The fact that we have written 63 with a .0 makes it a real number. It has a smaller part. It just so happens, its smaller part is a zero.

3. Variables

Variables are another thing that you encountered in your early days of arithmetic, math, or algebra. A variable is a place holder for a value. In fact when we first learned about variables we used boxes or ovals to represent place holders.

$$3 + \square = 7$$

In this case the □ meant that a value stood in this place of the box and you had to determine what the value was. This placeholder is a kind of variable. A variable can take on many values. That is its purpose.

Later on, in algebra the boxes went away and you were given expressions with things called variables.

$$3 + x = 7$$

In this case the "x" was the symbol standing for a variable. The variable x could take on any value you wanted to assign to it.

Now in a programming language, variables have two purposes. First, variables can take on any value assigned to them provided just as you learned. But the second purpose, and perhaps the more important purpose is that a variable is a name for a place in the computer's memory. You can give names to places in the computer's memory. For example a simple name might be

x

and a more complex name might be

temperature

Both of these can be used as variables in an expression. When you name a place in memory and when you give that place a value (so far we haven't given any values), the computer will remember the value you gave for that place in memory until the next time you change it. This capability, to remember things for you, turns out to be pretty useful as you learn to program a computer. It is especially useful when you are being the computer.

4. An expression also has operators. An operator specifies how the expression should be evaluated. When we write

3+4

the plus sign tells us to evaluate the expression by adding the two numbers together. The purpose of the operator is to specify what to do with the constants or variables in the expression. In C++ there are many operators. There are the arithmetic operators:

+
-
* (multiply)
/ (divide)

There are operators that you can use to compare two numbers:

< (less than)
<= (less then or equal to)
> greater than
>= greater than or equal to
== exactly equal to
!= not equal to

These are called the comparative operators. When using an operator to compare two numbers the result of that comparison can only be true or false. Consider the expression,

5 < 7.

The result of this expression will always be true.

On the other hand, consider the expression,

5 > 7.

The result of this expression will always be false.

Finally, as a third example, consider the expression,

5 == 5.

The result of this expression will also always be true.

The word "true" and the word "false" are special values. They are like the number values we have referred to earlier that in this case they are each represented by a word – either "true" or "false." These special values have a type associated with them. They are called logical or Boolean values. The reason for this is that they are used in other expressions that involve the same kinds of values. This is a very important point. A logical value cannot be used in an arithmetic expression. We cannot say,

5 + false

It is an expression that does not make sense. What would its result be? Actually it does not have a result. We would say that the result of this expression when evaluated is undefined. Likewise, arithmetic operators cannot be used with logical values. The expression,

5 + false

makes no sense because + (addition) is not defined for numeric values and logical values.

The lesson here is that we need to be careful when we construct expressions to be evaluated because, some expressions cannot be mixed. Different types cannot be used in the same expression.

The logical or Boolean values have their own operators which are called the logical or Boolean operators. There are three of these in C++:

&&
||
!

&& is used to represent the operation named "and." || is used to represent the operation named "or" and ! is the symbol used to represent the logical operation named "not."

Each of these operations, and, or, and not comes with a table called a truth table. The purpose of the truth table is to define the result of an expression containing one or two operands of the logical type. For each operator there is a truth table. The three truth tables are shown below: one for the logical operation &&, one for the logical operation ||, and one for the logical operation !.

Logical Operation **Truth Table**

Logical Operation Truth table

&&

||

!

&&	true	false
true	true	false
false	false	false
||	true	false
true	true	true
false	true	false
!		
true	false	
false	true	

5. Punctuation

In an expression, if you remember from your algebra class, there is an order in which operations are carried out. If the operators in the expression are the same, the order of doing the operations is simply left to right.

1 + 4 + 9
Order:
1 + 4 = 5
5 + 9 = 14

1 – 4 – 9
Order:
1 – 4 = -3
-3 – 9 = -12

If you have an expression like –

1 + 4 * 9 =
4 * 9 = 36
36 + 1 = 37

In the scheme of evaluating an expression with two different operators, the operators have what is called precedence. The precedence of two operators is determined by the rules of algebra. In this case the rules of algebra dictate that multiplication comes before addition and subtraction. So too does division come before addition and subtraction.

The punctuation that can be used in expressions are the left and right parenthesis. They are always used in a pair so as to enclose part of an expression. In terms of evaluation, an expression in parenthesis is evaluated before parts of the expression that are not inside of the parenthesis. Let's examine the previous expression but this time with punctuation.

(1 + 4) * 9 =
5 * 9 = 45

Notice how the parenthesis changes the value of the expression.

When using parenthesis care must be taken as to insure they are properly nested. Consider the following expression.

4 * 3 + 6 / 2 – 7 * 2

Evaluating the expression as it is written,

4 * 3 + 6 / 2 – 7 * 2 =
12 + 6 / 2 – 7 * 2 =
12 + 3 – 7 * 2 =
12 + 3 – 14 =
15 – 14 =
1

We will change the expression by adding a pair of parenthesis to it and then evaluate the expression again.

4 * (3 + 6) / 2 – 7 * 2 =
4 * 9 / 2 – 7 * 2 =
36 / 2 – 7 * 2 =
18 – 7 * 2 =
18 – 14 =
4

Here is another example of using punctuation to readjust the order of operations in the expression.

4 * (3 + 6) / ((2 – 7) * 2) =
4 * (3 + 6) / (-5 * 2) =

4 * (3 + 6) / -10 =
4 * 9 / -10 =
36 / -10 =
3.6

6. In the past examples you have seen how expressions are evaluated. Each of the examples shows expressions that are made up of constants. If an expression has variables as part of it, there is no difference in the evaluation except that the value of the variable must replace the variable in the expression.

Suppose we have the expression,

(4 * (3 + var1) / (var2 – 7) * var3) =

Before evaluating this expression we would have to know the values of

var1
var2
var3

Suppose var1 = 1, var2 = 2, and var3 = 3. We can rewrite our expression as follows.

(4 * (3 + 1) / (2 – 7) * 3) =

The evaluation of this expression is left to the reader as an exercise. (Remember to break this expression into smaller parts in order to carry out its evaluation).

Part 1 ______________________
Part 2 ______________________
Part 3 ______________________
Part 4 ______________________
Part 5 ______________________
Part 6 ______________________

Chapter 5
Our First Sentences in the C++ Language

You are now ready to write your first sentences in the C++ language. These sentences, albeit simple, are extremely important. They are used to identify the variables that your programs will use. Before any variable is used, it must be identified. This identification is called a DECLARATION. In order to use any variable in an expression it must be declared. A variable declaration consists of parts. The sentence for variable declaration consists of two words and punctuation.

As the name implies a declaration is a statement that makes an announcement. In this case what is being announced is that there is a memory location and the memory location can store data of a certain type. It used to be we had to know where the memory location was in memory. Now it is easier because we can name any memory location, and then use that name to refer to that memory location. Let's take a moment and consider what this might look like in the computer's memory. Suppose we want to compute the area of a rectangle. The formula for the area of a rectangle is

area = width x height

In this expression we are using 3 variables, area, width, and height. That means that each of these variables must be declared so that they are attached to places in memory. In other words, give the variables a home in memory where the variables, and their values will reside. This residence is called a location. We say that a variable is assigned to or allocated to a location in memory.

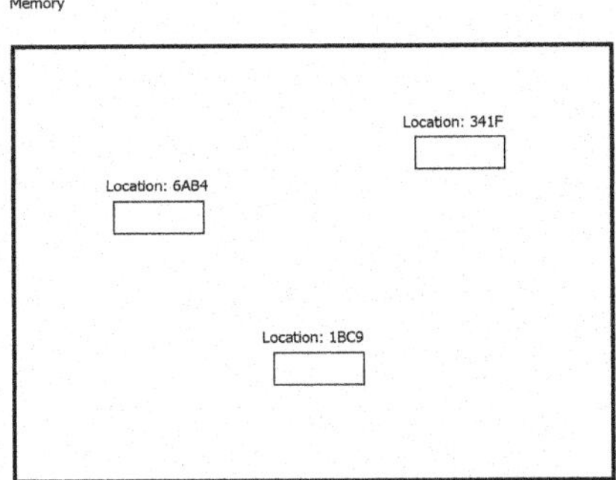

Here is a slice of memory with three locations. Most computer memory has billions of locations like these three. Our example of locations suffices to show what we need in our example. Notice the locations are empty. That is because we haven't done anything to the locations. We haven't stored any data in these locations. Now we will reserve these locations for the data we need to store and we will also name the three locations.

```
int width;
int height;
int area;
```

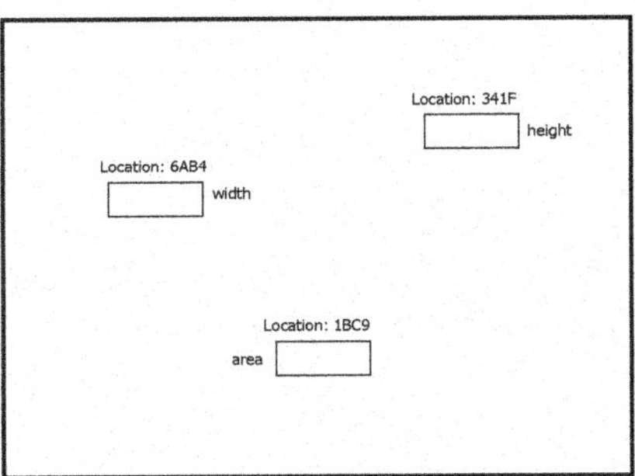

Short Review

1. What is the name of location 1BC9?
2. Where is the variable height assigned in memory?
3. What is the location of width?

Imagine that you can look into memory to see where things are and what they are called. We can't usually do this but we can imagine it. In our case the computer assigned the name height to the address 341F. This is where the value of the height variable will be stored. At location 6AB4 the value of the width variable will be stored. And finally at 1BC9, the value of the variable area will be stored.

We can assign values to these locations using an assignment sentence, the name of the variable, and a value.

width = 7 inches*
height = 9 inches*
area = 7 inches x 9 inches = 63 square inches.*

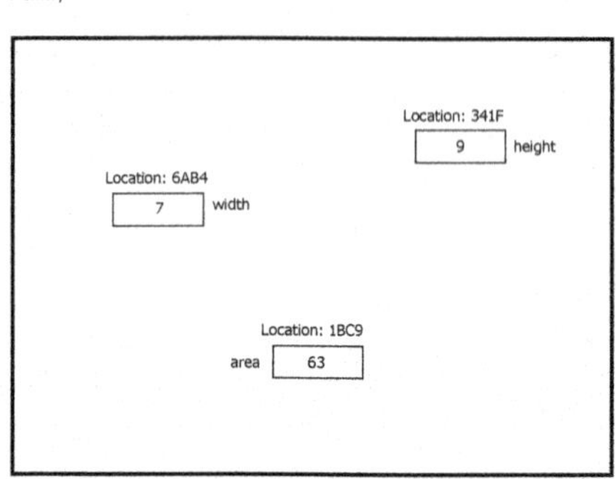

And that is pretty much it. Variables are declared, and then given a value, which is then stored at the variable's location in memory.

In our example we've given three examples of declarations.

```
int width;
int height;
int area;
```

Each of these is a sentence in the language C++. They are declaration sentences.

* I have included these labels to clarify their meaning. They are not part of the declaration sentence.

The first word in a declaration sentence is called a data type. A data type is a special word that specifies the kind of variable that is being declared. A variable "kind" is the type of value it can hold. This concept was reviewed earlier. For example, if you declare a variable to be an integer then the value of that variable must always be an integer. An integer value is a whole number without a decimal portion (a portion smaller than 1).

The second word of the declaration sentence is the name of the variable (the name of the memory location) you are declaring (reserving) for some data. We are declaring 3 variables:

width
height
area

This is a very short sentence. Only two words. There are sentences in English with only two words. For example, "Go there." is one example of a two-word English sentence.

So what exactly can be used as the first word in a declaration sentence. Here are some of the words (also called types) that you can use and what they mean.

First word of a declaration sentence	**Meaning**
int	Declares the name that follows as an integer (a whole number)
float	Declares the name that follows as a real number. Only 1 unit of space is reserved for float numbers
Double	Declares the name that follows as a real number. Two units of space is reserved for double numbers
Char	Declares the name that follows as a single character. A character is basically any one character you can type on your keyboard.

Section Exercise

For each of the following, write a sentence in C++ that is the C++ version of the English sentence.

For example, write a sentence in C++ that declares the variable name alpha as an integer.

Example(Answer) int alpha;

1. Write a sentence in C++ that declares the variable pi as a 1 memory unit real number.

2. Write a sentence in C++ that declares the variable x as an integer.

3. Write a sentence in C++ that declares the variable y as a 2 memory unit real number.

4. Write a sentence in C++ that declares t as a two memory unit real number.

5. Write a sentences in C++ that declares the variables name a, b, and c as integers.

The answer to the last exercise should have resulted in you writing three sentences.

```
int a;
int b;
int c;
```

This is very redundant. Isn't there a way we could express the same information in a variable of the declaration sentence?

There is a longer version of the declaration sentence. In the longer version of the declaration sentence you can have a list of variables that you wish to declare. The previous example could be written as:

```
int a, b, c;
```

and

```
int a;
int b;
int c;
```

which are equivalent.

Notice the use of a different punctuation character. The comma is used to separate multiple items in a list of items. This sentence says,

"Declare the variable a, b, and c to be integer variables."

It is extremely important to be able to paraphrase a sentence in C++ into a corresponding sentence in English (or whatever natural language you use to communicate). The reason for this is twofold.

First, if you can paraphrase a sentence in a programming language into English then you are demonstrating what the sentence does. This is one way you can show you understand the C++ sentence.

Second, if you can paraphrase from the C++ sentenc to English then you should be able to write a C++ sentence from English for similar purposes.

This section is entitled, "Our First Sentences in the C++ language. So far you have learned one sentence, the declaration sentence in C++. The second sentence you will learn is the assignment sentence.

The declaration sentence in C++ only gives a name to a place in memory and specifies the type of data that memory will contain. An assignment sentence lets you store data in the places in memory you have declared with a declaration sentence.

In English the assignment statement says,

> "Assign the calculated value of the expression on the right hand side of the equals sign to the location in memory reserved for the variable on the left hand side of the equals sign."

Remember that an expression is a phrase in a sentence whose value can be evaluated, or computed, or calculated from the expression. The simplest expression would be a number. For example,

7
451
32
1

are all examples of expressions. The first expression has the value 7, the second 451, the third 32, and the last has the value 1.

We wish to declare the variable r as an integer and then assign the value of the expression 7 to this variable.

```
int r;
r = 7;
```

These are the sentences that accomplishes this. At the end of following these instructions a memory location is reserved for the variable r as an integer and then the value of the expression 7 is stored at the location reserved for the variable r in memory.

One of the things that we wish to learn to do is to keep track of the contents of the memory locations associated with variables. To accomplish this, we create a way to record the contents of memory locations. A memory location will be represented by a rectangle and the rectangle will be labeled with variable name whose value we are keeping track of.

r	7

This is the representation of the C++ sentences,

```
int r;
r = 7;
```

Let's add another sentence to this sequence. We will add another assignment sentence to the sequence.

```
int r;
r = 7;
r = 15;
```

	15
r	7

We can use this method to keep track of the value of r as it changes. As for the surrogate for the computer you need to keep track of the contents of variables and their locations.

Summary

In this section you learned two sentences in the C++ language. One of these sentences is called the declaration sentence and the other is the assignment sentence. The declaration sentence is used to name and reserve a location in memory for a variable. The assignment sentence is used to store a value at the location designated by the variable name on the left hand side of the = sign. The right hand side of the assignment sentence is an expression that can be evaluated.

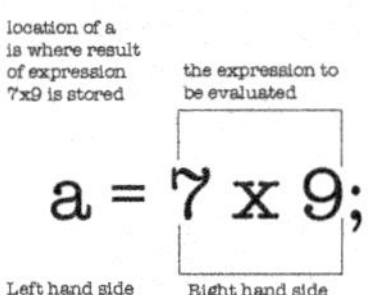

Section Exercise

1. Declare three variable i, j, k as integers in a single declaration sentence.
2. Declare three variables x, y, and z as doubles in three individual declaration sentences.

3. Declare a variable one as an integer and assign to it the value 0.

4. In another assignment sentence add 5 to the value of the variable one.

5. In a third assignment sentence subtract 2 from the value of the variable one.

6. In a diagram like the one shown earlier used to keep track of a variable, show the value of the variable one as its value changes from assignment sentence to assignment sentence.

7. Use a declaration sentence to declare a variable e as a double.

8. Use a declaration sentence to declare a variable r as a double.

9. Using an assignment sentence assign the value of r to 8.

10. Using an assignment sentence assign the value of e to the following expression.

$$(r * r) - (r + 3) * (r - 3)$$

a. Write the assignment sentence that assigns the variable e to thie value of this expression.
b. What is the value of e from the assignment sentence?

11. Draw a picture depicting the locations and values of each of the following statements. Assume the address of the first variable location is 0 and each subsequent location is the previous location + 4.

Simple declarations and assignments

If a variable is declared but not assigned use the symbol ⌧ to denote that the contents of the location is unassigned.

a. int a;
b. int a, b;
   a = 7;
   b = 9;
c. float a;
d. float x;
   x = 3.141;
   x = x * 2;
e. int x;
   x = 3.141 * 2;
f. double u;
   double v;
   double w;
   w = 3 * 1;
   u = w * 2;
   v = v * 7;

Strings

There is a kind of data that is very useful when writing any computer program. This kind of data is used for displaying written information when a computer runs a program. To be totally clear the term "runs" has a special meaning when it comes to programs and programming. It will be your job to follow the instructions of the program you write and do what those instructions say to do. The term that is used synonymously with "follow the instructions" is "run." When we say "run" a program we mean that we are following the instructions of the program and doing what the instructions say to do (as we simulate the computer actions).

A string is a sequence of characters – to begin with any characters that can be typed on the keyboard. Just as there are numeric constants as shown earlier there are also string constants. A string constant is a sequence of characters enclosed in quotation marks. Here are some examples of string constants.

"Here is an example of a string constant."
"abcdefghijklmnopqrstuvwxyz"
"stop"
"go"

And some examples of non-strings.

xyzw	(no quotation marks)
"wwwwww	(missing ending quotation marks)
eeeedddaaaa"	(missing quotation mark at the beginning of the string)
"a word" string"	a quotation mark in the middle of the string

We have introduced some of the numerical data types. There is also a string data type. To declare a variable to be a string data type we use the word "string" to start a declaration sentence. Examples:

string title;	Declare the variable title as a string variable
string x, y, z;	Declare the variables x, y, and z as string variables

One of the uses of a string variable or constant is to label output that is displayed. Output is displayed using a new kind of C++ sentence. Output is displayed on the input/output device. Most of the time, the output device is the display that is attached to the computer that you are using. Since I am using a laptop computer, the output device is the display attached to the laptop computer.

The following is an excerpt from an actual program containing the cout sentence.

```
{
    cout << "Here is an example of an output sentence";
}
```

After running the program, the display will look as follows:

```
Here is an example of an output sentence
```

In the larger context of the display, here is what this would look like.

The Output Sentence

```
Randys-MacBook-Air:~ rkaplan$ g++ simpleStringExample.cpp
Randys-MacBook-Air:~ rkaplan$ ./a.out
Here is an example of an output sentenceRandys-MacBook-Air:~ rkaplan$
```

The output sentence begins with the special word "cout." The output sentence consists of 3 parts. The first part of course is the starting word cout, the second is the pair of symbols << (less than, less than), and the third part is the string to be output on the display. An example of the cout sentence would be

```
cout << "Here is an example of a cout sentence";
```

When this statement is run the result will be the string,

Here is an example of a cout sentence

(Don't forget the semi-colon to end the C++ sentence.)

An assignment statement can also be used with a string. That is to say the value of a string constant can be assigned to a string variable.

```
string s;
s = "A string constant";
cout << s;
```

will result is the output of the string

A string constant

Section Exercise

1. Write a string with the following text: The weather today will be rainy with a temperature of 65 degrees.

2. Assign the string "We just purchased a new automobile." to the string variable statement.

3. Write a sentence to display the string variable sentence defined in exercise 2.

4. Write a sequence of C++ sentences that will display a sequence of strings

```
string 1
string 2
string 3
string 4
string 5
string 6
string 7
string 8
string 9
string 10
```

Write this sequence so that the string constant "string" need only be specified once and used in the output sentences.

Hint 1: you can output a sequence of strings and variables using multiple << symbols in the output sentence. Example:

```
string restOfString;
restOfString = " the rest of the string";
cout << "Here is a string with " << restOfString;
```

Hint 2: There is a special string that you can use to cause the output to proceed to a new line. Without using this special string, all of the output will occur on the same line. The special string is "\n".

Summary

A string constant is a sequence of characters such as those you can type on the computer's keyboard. One that denotes the beginning of the string and one that denotes the end of the string.

A string constant is always enclosed in quotation marks. Never forget either of these quotation marks.

A string constant can be assigned to a variable that is declared as a string variable using a C++ assignment sentence.

A string constant can be displayed using a C++ cout sentence.

A string variable can be displayed using a C++ cout sentence.

A cout sentence consists of the starting word cout, followed by the symbol <<, and then the string constant or variable.

Multiple items can be displayed by joining them together with the << symbol as in,

```
cout << “This is a string” << restOfString;
```

A new line can be output between strings by inserting the special string “\n”.

Summary of C++ sentences learned so far.

1. Declaration sentence
   Example:
   ```
   int i;
   double f;
   string str;
   ```

2. Assignment sentence
   Example:
   ```
   i = 0;
   f = 3.141;
   str = “one two three”;
   ```

3. Output sentence:
   Example:

```
cout << "The value of i is ";
cout << "The value of i is " << i;
cout << str << "\n";
int r;
r = 3;
cout << "The value of the expression r * r * (r + r) is " <<
        r * r * (r + r) << "\n";
```

The Input Sentence

We have shown, although not explicitly, how data can be input to the computer. We can use the assignment sentence to assign a value to a variable. By doing this, we are placing a value in memory associated with the variable name given to that location in memory. This approach would require the user of your program to know a little something about programming to get their data into the computer. They would have to know which assignment sentence to change to get that value into the program and also how to change that assignment sentence to obtain that desired result. This is a possibility although a complex one for the person using your program. One of the things about computer programming is that certain things come in pairs. There is an output sentence so there must be an input sentence (Well, must is a strong word but I use it from experience). And in fact there is an input sentence. The input sentence in C++ happens to be very similar to the output sentence with a couple of minor changes.

Saying that the input sentence is paired with the output sentence gives you some hint as to what the input sentence might look like. In the output sentence there is a special word that begins the sentence, **cout**. In the input sentence there is a related word, **cin**.

In the output sentence there is a special symbol that follows, the <<. If you think about these as a kind of pointer it is showing the direction of the flow of data. The data will flow from the variable to the cout. cout is the "portal" through which data must be output in order to output the data on the display. If the << is the symbol to send data to the output. What would you guess is the symbol to get data as input?

As I said, statements usually come in pairs and if the output symbol is << then correspondingly the input symbol should be >> and in fact that is the symbol that specifies the direction of input. Of course it would not make much sense if the word used to begin the sentence is cout as this implies the the program is producing some sort of output. Again, **what** would you guess is the word for input?

If you guessed **cin** you would be correct. We have the beginning word of the input sentence and the symbols used in that sentence. All that remains is where to put the data once the data is received. Well in the case of the output sentence, when the data was to be output from a variable, the next item in the sentence was a variable name (in case output came from the variable). Data going into your program must go into memory, and the way that you access memory is with a variable name. Therefore, the input sentence must look something like:

```
cin >> aVariableName;
```

This is an example of an input sentence.

When using an input sentence in a program, when the computer runs that sentence it will seem to stop all activity. Why is that? Because when you use the input sentence the computer is waiting for you to input something. Until you do that the computer will sit and wait for some input to be entered using the keyboard.

What does this look like if you are going to be the computer? When you run an input statement, you wait until data is input. How can you get input data? Well you can make it like a game. Get someone to help you and whenever the program asks for input, have them tell you what the input should be. This is extremely useful when you are trying to figure out why a program does not work the way you expect it to work. If your partner gives you "bad" data, you will get to see what your computer does when it receives bad data from input. In this case "bad" data would be data that is unexpected or incorrect in some way.

There is a tendency for your input helper to do a number of different things when helping you to test your program by providing data. First they may opt to give you data that is all bad. Now you may not even check for bad data so your program may not do anything. You need to account for bad data and this is an important oversight when writing any computer program. On the other hand your helper may give you only good data. This is not the nest situation either. If you always receive data that is good, how will you know if you can handle bad data? Your helper should always give a mixture of good and bad data. One way to insure this is not to tell your helper anything about the data you need. Of course this may lead to some really off-the-wall data, but that in itself is not a bad thing. Keep this in mind when you are enlisting your data helpers.

Let's write a small program, a series of sentences, that use both the input and output sentences.

```
int inputData;

cout << "Please input a number from 1 to 10: ";
cin >> inputData;

cout << "The number that you input was " <<
        inputData << "\n";
```

Now run this program as if you were the computer.

The first sentence, int inputData causes what to happen?

If you answered that it causes a memory location to be allocated with the name inputData that would be correct. At this point in time, memory would look as shown below.

inputData

Notice that the memory location is empty. This is because we've put nothing into the memory location yet. This is about to change.

The next thing you will see is an output string created by the output statement,

```
cout << "Please input a number from 1 to 10: ";
```

The string will be displayed on the monitor and it will look as follows.

Please input a number from 1 to 10:

This string is called a **PROMPT**. It is called that because it alerts whoever is running the program that they are expected to input a number from 1 to 10. Since you are being the computer and as the user you will enter a number (or imagine you are) from 1 to 10.

The next sentence of this program waits for the value that will be entered via the keyboard.

Here the user of the program is expected to enter a number from 1 to 10. Let's enter a 6. This means memory will change accordingly.

inputData	6

‡

As you can see, after the 6 has been entered it gets stored in the memory location associated with the variable inputData.

Finally, to see what was entered another cout sentence is used. This cout sentence outputs a string and also the value contained in the variable inputData.

The number that you input was 6 (newline)

Newline is to indicate that the display is advanced to the next line, a newline. Taken altogether, the program and its trace of memory looks as follows.

‡ One of the questions that often arises at this time is how does cin know what kind of data it should be looking for? Should it be looking for an integer? A double? Or a string? In most cases cin has access to the data type of the variable so it can know what type of input it needs to get when called upon.

Sentence	Memory	Input/Output
cout "Please input a number from 1 to 10: ";	inputData [ ]	Please input a number from 1 to 10:
cin >> inputData;	inputData [ ]	6
cin >> inputData;	inputData [6]	
cout << "The number that was input was " << inputData << "\n";	inputData [6]	The number input was 6 (newline)

The table shown above is a representation of what occurs within the computer to carry out the steps that make up the program. Correspondingly, here is what the program looks like when a computer runs the program.

```
{
  int inputData;

  cout << "Please enter a number from 1 to 10: ";
  cin >> inputData;
  cout << "The number that was input was " << inputData  << "\n";

}
```

And running the program yields the following:

```
Please enter a number from 1 to 10: 6
The number that was input was 6
```

Summary

Types of sentences in a programming language sometimes come in pairs. This is especially true if there are related but opposite functions as is the case with input and output.

The sentence to output data to the display begins with cout and the sentence to input data from the keyboard is cin.

The cout sentence will output whatever follows the << symbol to the display. Multiple things can be displayed, each item separated by from one another by <<.

The cin sentence will result in a pause of the program where the computer is awaiting input. The symbol used in this sentence is a >> and the item used is a variable name where the data will be stored once it is entered.

Section Exercise

1. Explain what the following sentence does. Assume the variable z has been declared as an integer.

```
cin >> z;
```

2. What is incorrect about the following sequence of sentences?

```
cout << “The value of the variable x is :”;
cout << x << “\n”;
```

3. For the following prepare a code trace table as prepared earlier to show what happens when the program is run (by you). In other words, write down what goes on in your head as you follow the instructions in the program in order to simulate a computer running the program.

```
int j;
int k;
int m;

cout << “Here we are going to examine j, k, and m as
the program runs” << “\n”;

j = 0;
k = 0,
l = 0;
```

```
cout << "The value of j, k, and m, are respectively " <<
j << " " << k << " " << m << \n";

j = 1;
k = j + 2;
m = j + k + 4;

cout << "The new value of j is: << " " << j << "\n";
cout << "The new value of k is: << " " << k << "\n";
cout << "The new value of m is: << " " << m << "\n";

j = 2;
k = k * 2;
m = k * 2;

cout << "The new value of j, k, and m are respectively "
<< j << " " << k << " " << m << "\n";
```

In the next chapter we will introduce an entirely new sentence in C++. This sentence is different from those we have seen so far in that this sentence lets us change the order in which statements are executed by the computer.

Chapter Exercise

1. Explain exactly what happens when program sentences like the following are executed by the computer.

   a. int x,y;

   b. x = 2;

   c. y = x + 4;

2. A data type like **int** specifies ____________________________________.

3. Which of the following symbols along with the proper keyword causes input to occur? << or >>?

4. Supposing the computer is executing a cin statement and suppose that the data encountered by the cin statement is not of the expected type. What happens?

5. The function of the special words ________________ and ________________ carry out the ____________________ and ______________________ tasks in C++.

Chapter 6
Conditional Statements

There are two characteristics that distinguish computers from any other machine that has been created by humans. Computers can make decisions. Being able to make decisions is useful for several reasons including writing programs that can vary their behavior depending on the value of various variables in memory and the evaluations of expressions as they are computed. Up until now we have seen that the sentences in a program are executed one after another in a sequential fashion. But they don't have to be executed in this way. We can vary the order of execution by using a conditional sentence. Let's consider a very abstract example of this.

Suppose I have a formula where the denominator can be a number that is greater than or equal to 0. In other words, the number dividing can be a 0 or some other positive number. Everyone knows that we cannot divide any number by zero. The result will "blow up." If left unchecked the program, we write will fail. We say that the value of any number divided by zero is undefined. We don't want this to happen and prefer to handle the problem before it happens. Let's look at some sentences in C++ that have this problem. Let's consider figuring out the size of a slice of pie when the pie is divided into a specified number of pieces. Here are some sentences that will calculate this.

```
(1) int pieces;
(2) int  pieceSize;
(3) int pieSize; // The circumference of the pie
(4) int radius;
(5) cout << "How many pieces do you want to cut our of the pie? "
(6) cin >> pieces;
(7) cout << "What is the radius of the pie? "; // We can compute the
                                              // circumference from
                                              // the radius of the pie
(8) cin >> radius;

// Now compute the circumference

(9) pieSize = 2 * 3.14159 * radius;
```

```
// Now we can determine the size of each of the pieces of the pie

(10)   pieceSize = pieSize / pieces;

(11)   cout << "To get " << pieces << " cut each piece to " <<pieceSize;

(12)   cout << " measuring around the circumference. \n";
```

From what we know about computers so far, we know that each of these sentences are executed in the order that they are given. A small comment is in order first.

You will notice that some of the lines, and some of the text following a sentence in the C++ language begins with a // (double /). This is a special symbol that tells the compiler to ignore whatever follows the //. // is used to designate a comment in the program. A comment is something that another person may read in order to understand what the meaning of a certain sentence in a C++ program. Comments are there for humans to understand a program sentence or paragraph. This is really useful if you are new to the programming language and programming in general because it represents your thoughts about the sentence

Now it is your turn to "be the computer." Execute each of these statements and show the results of the statement in the following table.

Statement #	**Statement**	**Description of the statement**	**Variables**	**Variable Results** (after the statement is executed)	**Output**
1	Create the variable pieces	Create pieces and allocate space in memory for pieces	No value change here	No change	None
2	Create the variable pieceSize	Create pieceSize and allocate space in memory for pieces	No value change here	No change	None
3	Create the variable pieSize	Create pieSize and allocate space in memory for piece	No value change here	No change	None
4	Create the variable radius	radius and allocate space in memory for piece	No value change here	No change	None

Statement #	Statement	Description of the statement	Variables	Variable **Results** (after the statement is executed)	Output
5	cout << "How many pieces do you want to cut our of the pie? "	Output a prompt for the number of pieces to cut the pie into.			How many pieces do you want to cut our of the pie?
6	cin >> pieces	Have the user enter the number of pieces rhey wish to cut the pie into	pieces	pieces value	
7	cout << "What is the radius of the pie?"	Output a prompt for the radius of the pie			What is the radius of the pie?
8	cin >> radius	The user will enter the radius of the pie	radius	radius value	
9	pieSize = 2 * 3.14159 * radius;	Compute the circumference of the pie	pieSize, radius	pieSize	
10	pieceSize = pieSize/pieces;	Compute the size of each piece	pieceSize, pieSize, pieces	pieceSize	
11	cout << "To get " << pieces << " cut each piece to " <<pieceSize;	Output the number of pieces and the size of each of the pieces	Pieces, pieceSize		To get value of pieces cut each piece to the value of pieceSize
12	cout << " measuring around the circumference. \n";	Output the remainder of the output statement			measuring around the circumference

This table shows what <u>will</u> happen at each sentence of the program. However, the table does not show what actually happens if you were to run this program. The table does serve a purpose because by making changes to cells of the table, specifically those cells that deal with specific variable values, we are able to see what happens when the program runs. Look at the next version of this table altered to show an example of data that is entered by the user.

Statement #	Statement	Description of the statement	Variables	Variable Results (after the statement is executed)	Output
1	Create the variable pieces	Create pieces and allocate space in memory for pieces	No value change here	Memory has no value	None
2	Create the variable pieceSize	Create pieceSize and allocate space in memory for pieces	Memory allocated	Memory has no value	None
3	Create the variable pieSize	Create pieSize and allocate space in memory for piece	Memory allocated	Memory has no value	None
4	Create the variable radius	radius and allocate space in memory for piece	Memory allocated	No change	None
5	cout << "How many pieces do you want to cut our of the pie? "	Output a prompt for the number of pieces to cut the pie into.			How many pieces do you want to cut our of the pie?
6	cin >> pieces	Have the user enter the number of pieces rhey wish to cut the pie into	Pieces	Pieces 8	
7	cout << "What is the radius of the pie?"	Output a prompt for the radius of the pie			What is the radius of the pie?
8	cin >> radius	The user will enter the radius of the pie	radius	radius 12	
9	pieSize = 2 * 3.14159 * radius;	Compute the circumference of the pie	pieSize, radius	radius = 12 pieSize = 75	
10	pieceSize = pieSize/pieces;	Compute the size of each piece	pieceSize, pieSize, pieces	pieSize = 75 pieceSize = 12 pieces = 6	
11	cout << "To get " << pieces << " cut each piece to " <<pieceSize;	Output the number of pieces and the size of each of the pieces	pieces, pieceSize	pieces =12 piecesize = 6	To get 12 cut each piece to 6
12	cout << " measuring around the circumference. \n";	The rest of the results output statement			measuring around the circumference

The final result of this program will be that each piece measured around the circumference should be approximately 6". Although I haven't indicated inches anywhere in the program, we assume that the measurements are in inches. If you wanted to be clearer about this, which lines would you change in the program to specify that the measurements are in inches. Here is the program, again, so that you can make a determination of the lines you would change.

```
(1) int pieces;
(2) int  pieceSize;
(3) int pieSize; // The circumference of the pie
(4) int radius;
(5) cout << "How many pieces do you want to cut our of the pie?
(6) cin >> pieces;
(7) cout << "What is the radius of the pie? "; // We can compute the
                                              // circumference from
                                              // the radius of the pie
(8) cin >> radius;

// Now compute the circumference

(9) pieSize = 2 * 3.14159 * radius;

// Now we can determine the size of each of the pieces of the pie

(10)   pieceSize = pieSize / pieces;

(11)   cout << "To get " << pieces << " cut each piece to " <<pieceSize;

(12)   cout << " measuring around the circumference. \n";
```

Line ________

Line ________

Hint: They are output sentences.

We are still not finished with this example. Supposing that the user accidentally enters a 0 for the number of pieces in line 6. In line 10 we will have a division by 0. This cannot be because as I said earlier a division by 0 will result in the program giving an error and stopping. You would like to handle this in a better way so that the program does not end on a bad input, but simply asks for another value that is correct.

Remember I said that the computer (and you as the computer) will follow the sentences in a program in the order that they are given. sentence (1) first, then sentence (2), then sentence (3), and so on until sentence (12). The computer and you cannot deviate from running the sentences sequentially unless directed to do so. We would like to do just that. Change the order that the sentences are run when the user enters a 0 where the number of pie pieces have the value 0.

This is where a new kind of sentence, the conditional sentence, comes into the picture. A conditional sentence allows us to change in what sequence the sentences run. A different sequence is based on the evaluation of a conditional expression. For our program the condition that we are interested in is when pieces has the value 0.

The conditional sentence begins with the word **if**, followed by a conditional expression, followed by one or more sentences to run if the condition is true. The if-sentence in general looks like:

if (condition(s)) {statement(s)};

A condition is another kind of expression. There are two kinds of operators that can be used in a conditional expression. One kind of these are called comparative operators. As the name implies they allow you to write an expression that compares two numbers, or a variable, and a number or two variables. Remember the result of any comparative operator is TRUE or FALSE.

Here is the list of conditional operators. Which do you think we would use to test for our condition?

<	less than
<=	less than or equal to
==	exactly equal to
>=	greater than or equal to
>	greater than
!=	not equal to

We want to check to see if pieces is exactly the value of zero. Which operator would we use? If you chose == you would be correct.

We can write a condition that we will need as:

(pieces == 0)

If the value of pieces is zero, then this expression gets evaluated and has the value of true. Otherwise if the value of pieces is not zero, the value of this expression will be false.

The next thing to do is to decide what we want to do if the value of pieces is zero. Right now we will tell the user that they cannot enter 0 for the number of pieces. Later on we will change this so the user can re-enter pieces.

The sentences to tell the user that their input for pieces is incorrect and the program will be ended are:

```
cout << "Pieces must be a number greater than zero\n";
cout << "The program will end now. You can rerun the program
            to enter a correct value for pieces\n";
return 0;
```

The last sentence, return 0, tells the computer to stop running the program. More about the return sentence and what it does later in the book. Let's add this code to the program to see what the whole program looks like with these changes.

```
int pieces;
int pieceSize;
int pieSize; // The circumference of the pie
int radius;
cout << "How many pieces do you want to cut our of the pie?
cin >> pieces;

// This code checks to make sure that pieces is not zero

if (pieces == 0)
{
cout << "Pieces must be a number greater than zero\n";
cout << "The program will end now. You can rerun the program
                        to enter a correct value for pieces\n";
return 0;
}

cout << "What is the radius of the pie? "; // We can compute the
                                           // circumference from
                                           // the radius of the pie
cin >> radius;

// Now compute the circumference

pieSize = 2 * 3.14159 * radius;
```

```
// Now we can determine the size of each of the pieces of the pie

(18) pieceSize = pieSize / pieces;

(19) cout << "To get " << pieces << " cut each piece to " <<pieceSize;

(20) cout << " measuring around the circumference. \n";
```

Let's examine the flow of this program when pieces is zero and when pieces is not zero.

```
(1)  int pieces;
(2)  int pieceSize;
(3)  int pieSize; // The circumference of the pie
(4)  int radius;
(5)  cout << "How many pieces do you want to cut our of the pie?
(6)  cin >> pieces;

(7)  // This code checks to make sure that pieces is not zero

pieces > 0
(8)  if (pieces == 0)    evaluation of expression will be true
(9)  {
(10) cout << "Pieces must be a number greater than zero\n";
(11) cout << "The program will end now. You can rerun the program
(12)                         to enter a correct value for pieces\n";
(13) return 0;
(14) }

(15) cout << "What is the radius of the pie? "; // We can compute the
                                                // circumference from
                                                // the radius of the pie
(16) cin >> radius;

// Now compute the circumference

(17) pieSize = 2 * 3.14159 * radius;

// Now we can determine the size of each of the pieces of the pie

(18) pieceSize = pieSize / pieces;

(19) cout << "To get " << pieces << " cut each piece to " <<pieceSize;

(20) cout << " measuring around the circumference. \n";
```

Following the arrows a line 8 we see that if pieces is greater than 0 then the code from lines 9 through 14 are skipped. The cause of this "jump" is line 8 caused by the value of pieces being non-zero. Now let's look at the flow when pieces is 0.

```
int pieces,
int pieceSize;
int pieSize; // The circumference of the pie
int radius;
cout << "How many pieces do you want to cut our of the pie?
cin >> pieces;

// This code checks to make sure that pieces is not zero

pieces == 0   if (pieces == 0)  evaluation of expression will be false
{
cout << "Pieces must be a number greater than zero\n";
cout << "The program will end now. You can rerun the program
                          to enter a correct value for pieces\n";
return 0;                                          Exit the program
}
```

```
cout << "What is the radius of the pie? "; // We can compute the
                                           // circumference from
                                           // the radius of the pie
cin >> radius;

// Now compute the circumference

pieSize = 2 * 3.14159 * radius;

// Now we can determine the size of each of the pieces of the pie

pieceSize = pieSize / pieces;

cout << "To get " << pieces << " cut each piece to " <<pieceSize;

cout << " measuring around the circumference. \n";
```

This part of the program is ignored

Notice that because pieces is 0, the sentences inside the braces are executed and then the program is caused to stop by the return 0 sentence. The rest of the program is ignored. The "flow" was interrupted by this conditional sentence.

The implications of being able to change the order of the instructions executed is quite significant. Now, a machine can determine which instructions it is going to execute according to the value of one of more variables.

Let's consider another example. Suppose you had a variable named counter. Counter is an integer. And let's also suppose we have a series of if statements that test the value of counter. For each different value we would like to select one action to take. For example, if counter is equal to 1 then we want to do something because counter equals 1. If counter equals 2 then we want to do something else because counter has the value 2. If counter equals 3 then we want to do something else because counter has the value 3. This would look something like the following series of if-statements.

```
if (counter == 1)
{
        // do something when counter equals 1
}
if (counter == 2)
{
        // do something when counter equals 2
}
if (counter == 3)
{
        // do something when counter equals 3
}
```

When counter is 1, we want to add 1 to counter, and when counter equals 2 we also want to add one to counter. Here is what the conditional sentences will look like to achieve this.

```
counter = 1;
if (counter == 1)
{
        // do something when counter equals 1
        counter=counter+1;
}
if (counter == 2)
{
        // do something when counter equals 2
        counter=counter+1;
}
if (counter == 3)
{
        // do something when counter equals 3
}
```

When we begin this sequence of sentences we begin with the value of counter equal to 1.

The first condition of the first conditional sentence will be true at this point, so the code inside the braces increments (adds 1 to counter). This will make counter

= 2. Now the next statement tests to see if counter is 2, and it will be so the code inside the next set of braces will be executed.

This is not what we wish to happen though. If counter is 1, then we want to execute the first bunch of code (when the condition counter == 1) is true. After this code is executed we do not want count checked again until we are finished processing count with its new value. We want to skip over the rest of the if sentences in this group of if sentence. A second, slightly different version, of the if-sentence allows us to do just that.

The sentence is called an if-else statement. We can use the if-else sentence to circumvent the situation we described.

```
counter = 1;
if (counter == 1)
{
        // do something when counter equals 1
        i=i+1;
}
else if (counter == 2)
{
        // do something when counter equals 2
        i=i+1;
}
else if (counter == 3)
{
        // do something when counter equals 3
}
```

The difference between this version and the previous version of the code is the effect that the else-if sentence has.

Assume once more that counter is initialized to the value 1. The condition (counter == 1) would be true so the code in the braces with be executed. The variable i will be incremented by 1. The updated value of the variable i is now 2. Since the condition of the first if-sentence is true, none of the other if-sentences will be executed. The if-else sentence has the ability to cause no other if-sentence to be executed.

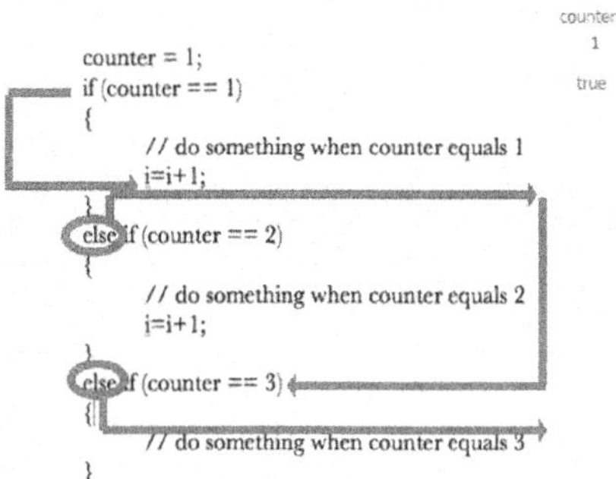

As you might imagine, if-sentences and if-else sentence can become very complex. To see this, let's write another program, so you can see the if-sentence in action.

Exercise

Before we proceed to the next example, let's have some practice with simple if-sentences. For each of the following if-sentences we will use the following variables and their corresponding values.

```
int x=0;
int y=6;
int z=7;
double pi=314159;
int year1=1902;
int year2=1952;
int year3=1982;
```

For each of the following if-sentences specify the result of the sentence.

1) Result: True/False   if (x > y) …
2) Result: True/False   if (x+y > z) …
3) Result: True/False   if (y+z>x) …
4) Result: True/False   if (2*pi>z) …
5) Result: True/False   if (year2-year1 > y*9) …
6) Result: True/False   if (year3-year1 > y*z*2) …

The purpose of the next program example is to play the game Tic-Tac-Toe. Your opponent will be the computer. This program will be much more complex than those you have seen so far, but you should still be able to understand what is happening in the program.

To begin we will consider the variables we will need to represent the tic-tac-toe board. We will need nine variables in all, one for each positon on the board. We will name the variables according to their position on the board. The type of variable we will use is an int type. We will use -1 to designate an O on the board and a +1 to designate an X on the board, while a 0 will denote that the space is empty (has not been used by a player yet). The variables are defined as follows and are also initialized.

```
int topLeft = 0;
int topCenter = 0;
int topRight =0;
int centerLeft = 0;
int centerCenter = 0;
int centerRight = 0;
int bottomLeft = 0;
int bottomCenter = 0;
int bottomRight = 0;
bool playerWins = false;
bool opponentWins = false;
```

Each cell on the board will be identified by a number form 1 to 9. The cells will be numbered from the top left through the bottom right, left to right and top to bottom as shown below.

1	2	3
4	5	6
7	8	9

A player would select a move (cell) by specifying the number of the cell in which to move. If they wished to move into the center, this could be specified by selecting cell 5. From the standpoint of writing a complete program to play Tic-Tac-Toe we really don't know everything we need to know in order for us to write all of the necessary sentences. Nevertheless, we can demonstrate how complex if sentences can be written to determine if one of the players has won the game.

In order to determine if one of the players has one the game after a move we need to check each row of the Tic-Tac-Toe board and then each column. Finally we have to check the diagonals of the board. First we will write the if-sentences for the rows. We have two sets of checks we must make, one to check if the player has taken a row and the other to check when the opponent has taken the row. (By taken the row we mean that they have filled the row with their mark).

We said earlier that a 1 in a cell would mean the player placed an X in the cell. Here is the if sentence to check the first row to see if the row is filled with X's.

Question

Why do I check to see if the value is a 1?

```
if ((topLeft == 1) && (topCenter == 1) && (topRight ==1))
        playerWins = true;
```

In our list of variable declarations, we've include two Boolean variables. A Boolean variable is a variable whose value can be true or false. This if sentence reads (in English) as follows.

If the top left most cell has an X and the top center cell has an X, and the top right cell has an X, then the player wins the game. The word "and" used here is actually a logical connective being used to join the individual expressions to check the cells in a row. Remember I said that there are two kinds of operators whose results are TRUE or FALSE. The comparatives are one type of operation while the logical connectives are the other. The logical connectives consist of the operators && (and), | | (or), and ! (not).

We will now write the remaining if sentences determine if the player or the opponent has won the game

```
// Check the Player
// Player wins on filling a row

        if ((topLeft == 1) && (topCenter == 1) && (topRight ==1))
                playerWins = true;
        else if ((centerLeft == 1) && (centerCenter == 1) && (centerRight ==1))
                playerWins = true;
        else if ((bottomLeft == 1) && (bottomCenter == 1) && (bottomRight ==1))
                playerWins = true;

        // Player wins on filling a column

        else if ((topLeft == 1) && (centerLeft == 1) && (bottomLeft == 1))
                playerWins = true;
        else if ((topCenter == 1) && (centerCenter == 1) && (bottomCenter == 1))
                playerWins = true;
        else if ((topRight == 1) && (centerRight == 1) && (bottomRight == 1))
                playerWins = true;

        // Player wins on filling a diagonal

        else if ((topLeft == 1) && (centerCenter== 1) && (bottomRight == 1))
                playerWins = true;
        else if ((topRight == 1) && (centerCenter == 1) && (bottomLeft == 1))
                playerWins = true;

// Check the Opponent
// Opponent wins on filling a row

        if ((topLeft == -1) && (topCenter == -1) && (topRight == -1))
                opponentWins = true;
        else if ((centerLeft == -1) && (centerCenter == -1) && (centerRight == -1))
                opponentWins = true;
        else if ((bottomLeft == -1) && (bottomCenter == -1) && (bottomRight
                == -1))
                opponentWins = true;

        // Opponent wins on filling a column

        else if ((topLeft == -1) && (centerLeft == -1) && (bottomLeft == -1))
```

```
        opponentWins = true;
else if ((topCenter == -1) && (centerCenter == -1) &&
        (bottomCenter == -1))
        opponentWins = true;
else if ((topRight == -1) && (centerRight == -1) && (bottomRight == -1))
        opponentWins = true;

// Oppoent wins on filling a diagonal

else if ((topLeft == -1) && (centerCenter == -1) && (bottomRight == -1))
        opponentWins = true;
else if ((topRight == -1) && (centerCenter == -1) && (bottomLeft == -1))
        opponentWins = true;
```

Question

Why do I check to see if the value of the cell is a -1?

Let's now look at how these sentences work to test whether the player or the opponent won. As before we begin with a table showing the variables that are part of the program paragraph containing the if-sentences.

t-	topLeft	topCenter	topRight	leftCenter	centerCenter
0	0	0	0	0	0

t-	rightCenter	leftBottom	centerBottom	rightBottom	player Wins	Opp Wins
0	0	0	0	0	0	0

When the program starts the sentences declaring the board variables and the sentences declaring who won the game are set to 0 and false respectively. (t-0)

Then some moves occur and we determine if the player or the opponent has won the game. At this point the board looks something like:

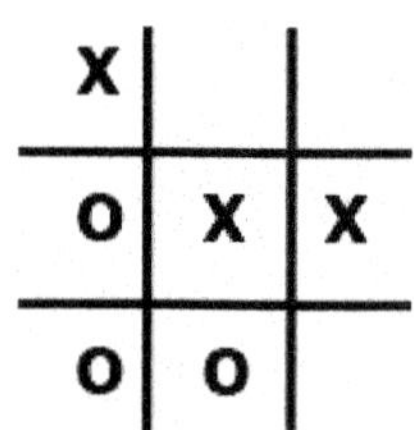

The table of variables would be updated accordingly.

t-	topLeft	topCenter	topRight	leftCenter	centerCenter
0	0	0	0	0	0
1	1	0	0	-1	1

t-	rightCenter	leftBottom	centerBottom	rightBottm	player Wins	Opp Wins
0	0	0	0	0	false	false
1	1	-1	-1	0		

We can go through each of the if-sentences to see if any of them are true thus indicating a winner.

In the if-sentences the expressions that are true are highlighted in green.

```
    if ((topLeft == 1) && (topCenter == 1) && (topRight ==1))
        playerWins = true;
    else if ((centerLeft == 1) && (centerCenter == 1) && (centerRight ==1))
        playerWins = true;
    else if ((bottomLeft == 1) && (bottomCenter == 1) && (bottomRight ==1))
        playerWins = true;

    // Player wins on filling a column

    else if ((topLeft == 1) && (centerLeft == 1) && (bottomLeft == 1))
        playerWins = true;
    else if ((topCenter == 1) && (centerCenter == 1) && (bottomCenter == 1))
        playerWins = true;
    else if ((topRight == 1) && (centerRight == 1) && (bottomRight == 1))
        playerWins = true;

    // Player wins on filling a diagonal

    else if ((topLeft == 1) && (centerCenter== 1) && (bottomRight == 1))
        playerWins = true;
    else if ((topRight == 1) && (centerCenter == 1) && (bottomLeft == 1))
        playerWins = true;

// Check the Opponent
// Opponent wins on filling a row

    if ((topLeft == -1) && (topCenter == -1) && (topRight == -1))
        opponentWins = true;
    else if ((centerLeft == -1) && (centerCenter == -1) && (center[Right == -1))
        opponentWins = true;
    else if ((bottomLeft == -1) && (bottomCenter == -1) && (bottomRight
        == -1))
        opponentWins = true;

    // Opponent wins on filling a column

    else if ((topLeft == -1) && (centerLeft == -1) && (bottomLeft == -1))
        opponentWins = true;
    else if ((topCenter == -1) && (centerCenter == -1) &&
        (bottomCenter == -1))
```

```
        opponentWins = true;
else if ((topRight == -1) && (centerRight == -1) && (bottomRight == -1))
        opponentWins = true;

// Opponent wins on filling a diagonal

else if ((topLeft == -1) && (centerCenter == -1) && (bottomRight == -1))
        opponentWins = true;
else if ((topRight == -1) && (centerCenter == -1) && (bottomLeft == -1))
        opponentWins = true;
```

As you can see there is no if-sentence whose 3 conditions are met (three green highlights in a row). Let's now add a player's move in the bottom right cell.

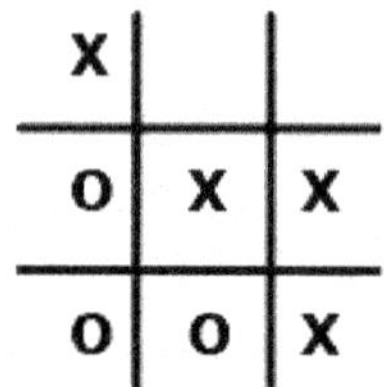

This additional move changes the variable tracking table shown.

	topLeft	topCenter	topRight	leftCenter	centerCenter
0	0	0	0	0	0
1	1	0	0	-1	1
2	1	0	0	-1	1

	rightCenter	leftBottom	centerBottom	rightBottm	player Wins	Opp Wins
0	0	0	0	0	false	false
1	1	-1	-1	0		
2	1	-1	-1	1		

Accordingly, one of the if-sentences is affected.

```
else if ((topLeft == 1) && (centerCenter== 1) && (bottomRight == 1))
        playerWins = true;
```

Now, this if-sentence contains the necessary true expressions therefore the variable playerWins will be set to true.

t-	topLeft	topCenter	topRight	leftCenter	centerCenter
0	0	0	0	0	0
1	1	0	0	-1	1
2	1	0	0	-1	1

	rightCenter	leftBottom	centerBottom	rightBottm	player Wins	Opp Wins
0	0	0	0	0	false	false
1	1	-1	-1	0		
2	1	-1	-1	1	true	

Expression and If-sentence Exercises

1. Assume that the following variables have the following values. (Determine if the value of the expression is true or false).

   int a = 1;
   int b = 2;
   int c = 3;

   int d;
   int f;

   double g = 2.1;
   double h = 10.0;
   double j = 3.14;

   Evaluate each of the following expressions.

   a) (1>2)
   b) (2>1>3)
   c) ((b*2) == c)
   d) ((b*2) == 4)
   e) (a>0)
   f) (a-1>0)
   g) d = 14; (d > (2*8))
   h) d = 14; ((2*8) > 2)

i) (j*j) == (2*j)
j) (a<=1)
k) (a>=2)
l) (a*3>=c*3)
m) (c != b)
n) (j<=h)
o) (h>(j*2)) && (c>a)
p) ((a+b) < 0)||(j >= j)
q) (j<h) && (j*h)<30||(h==g)
r) (a==1)&&(a!=1)
s) (true || false) && (false || false)
t) (true && false) || (true || false)

2. For each of the if-sentences specify whether the code in the braces {} will be executed.

```
int a = 1;
int b = 2;
int c = 3;

int d;
int f;

double g = 2.1;
double h = 10.0;
double j = 3.14;
```

a) if (a<b) {// do-something}
b) if(b<a) {// do-something}
c) if(b<a+2) {// do-something}
d) if((h*g) < (h*j) && ((a*b*c)*h > (j*j))){// do-something}

Chapter 7
Iteration

Besides being able to make decisions as to which code will run when, one more aspect of any programming language and also the computer that runs that programming language is something called "iteration."

You may never have heard of this word before, but the word basically means "to repeat." Computers can do the same operations again, and again without getting tired or sick and also produce the same results for the same data. That characteristic is also extremely important. A computer can repeat an operation (typically more than one operation) as many times as we wish it to repeat those operations. For example, if you want to do something 10 times, it is possible to do so in a program. If you want to do the same thing 1,000,000 times, it is also possible.

Just like the if-sentence there are three sentences that will allow you to write a sentence that iterates. These are the for-sentence, the while-sentence, and the do-while sentence. There are also two helper sentences that you will find useful and convenient to use under certain circumstances. Let's take a closer look at these sentences used for iteration.

Supposing we wanted to create a series of statements that was repeated 10 times. In other words, we wanted to do something 10 times. In English we might express this as

Repeat the following instructions 10 times { … }

We might want to have the computer output the word "Hello" 10 times as shown below.

Hello
Hello
Hello
Hello
Hello
Hello

Hello
Hello
Hello
Hello

That would look something like,

Repeat the following instructions 10 times { cout << "Hello"; }

The sentence we will use is the "while" sentence. What can we use to count? A variable can be used to keep track of the number of times we will output "Hello." Let's declare an integer "count" for this purpose. The variable "count" will first be initialized to 0.

(1) int count = 0;

Now we want to make sure that the count never exceeds 10. We can achieve this with the new sentence "while." Here's what that looks like.

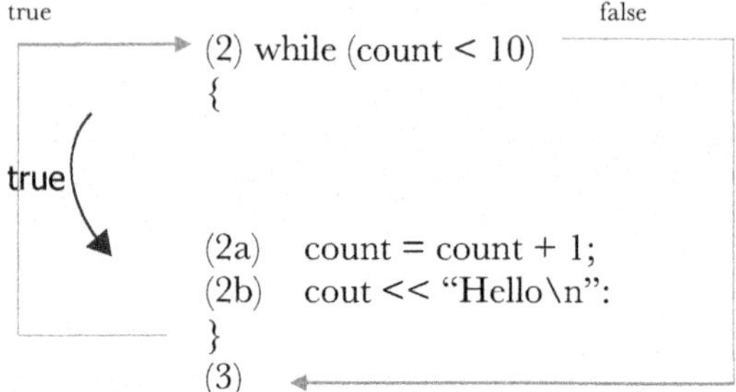

Like we've done before, let's trace this code as it runs. We've numbered the steps so we can keep track of what statement is being executed. The arrow shows what happens when we reach the enclosing brace. We return to the while sentence at step 2 and check the value of i again.

Step	Value of counter	Evaluate	Output
1	0		
2	0	(count < 10) → true	

Step	Value of i	Evaluate	Output
2a	1		
2b	1		Hello
2	1	(count < 10) ➔ true	
2a	2		
2b	2		Hello
2	2	(count < 10) ➔ true	
2a	3		
2b	3		Hello
2	3	(count < 10) ➔ true	
2a	4		
2b	4		Hello
2	4	(count < 10) ➔ true	
2a	5		
2b	5		Hello
2	5	(count < 10) ➔ true	
2a	6		
2b	6		Hello
2	6	(count < 10) ➔ true	
2a	7		
2b	7		Hello
2	7	(count < 10) ➔ true	
2a	8		
2b	8		Hello
2	8	(count < 10) ➔ true	
2a	9		
2b	9		Hello
2	9	(count < 10) ➔ true	
2a	10		
2b	10		Hello
2	10	(count < 10) ➔ false	
		At this point, when the condition evaluates to false, the loop ends	

This type of loop (remember I said there are three types) is called a while loop (as signified by the initial sentence word "while." The idea behind the while loop is that the iteration inside of the loop will continue until the condition of the loop becomes false.

In this example we used a while loop to demonstrate how a loop works. In actuality, a while loop is called a non-counting loop, which means there is no counter built into the loop. Another loop sentence, called the for-loop, is called a counting loop. It repeats code a certain number of times before it ends. Unlike a while loop though, the number of times is specified in the for-loop sentence.

The for-loop sentence is complex. So pay attention to the rules of writing this sentence.

```
for (initialize; condition; increment)
{
        ... code to repeat
}
```

A for-loop sentence that mimics the while-loop sentence example would be written as follows.

```
for (counter = 1; counter <= 10; counter = counter + 1)
{
        ... code to repeat
}
```

Notice that the for-loop sentence has three parts. Each part is separated from the next part with a semi-colon. At the end of the sentence is a closing right parenthesis.

This sentence says, with counter initialized to 1, so long as counter <= 10, do the code inside the loop, THEN increment the counter by 1. Let's make this code equivalent to the previous example this time using the for-loop sentence.

```
(1) for (counter = 1; counter <= 10; counter = counter + 1)
(2){
(2a)    cout << "Hello\n";
(3)}
(4) ... rest of the program ...
```

Notice that the step to increment the counter variable is no longer part of the loop because the for-sentence handles that part of the work for us. The trace of this version of the loop is shown in the next table.

Step	Value of i	Evaluate	Output
1	1	(counter <= 10) ➔ true	
2a	1		Hello
1	2	(counter <= 10) ➔ true	
2a	2		Hello
1	3	(counter <= 10) ➔ true	
2a	3		Hello
1	4	(counter <= 10) ➔ true	
2a	4		Hello
1	5	(counter <= 10) ➔ true	
2a	5		Hello
1	6	(counter <= 10) ➔ true	
2a	6		Hello
1	7	(counter <= 10) ➔ true	
2a	7		Hello
1	8	(counter <= 10) ➔ true	
2a	8		Hello
1	9	(counter <= 10) ➔ true	
2a	9		Hello
1	10	(counter <= 10) ➔ true	
2a	10		Hello
1	11	(counter <= 10) ➔ false	
4		loop ends and exits to statement 4 after the loop body	

The for-loop sentence is very versatile. For example, the loop variable can be incremented by any value.

```
for (counter = 1; counter <= 10; counter = counter + 2)
{
        ... code to repeat
}
```

Can you predict what the values of counter will be? Can you determine how many times the loop will be executed?

Likewise, it is possible to decrement the value of the counter. Of course for this to work properly, we also have to change the condition.

```
for (counter = 10; counter >= 1; counter = counter - 1)
{
        ... code to repeat
}
```

In fact, the increment part of the for-loop sentence could have any expression to which count will be updated.

A Brief Diversion

In the for-loop sentence, in the increment part of the sentence you will notice that the sentence is written with a full assignment statement (counter = counter – 1). Now C++ has some shorthand which is pretty useful and now is a good time to introduce it. You can increment a variable by using a special operator called the increment operator.

counter++

is equivalent to

counter = count + 1.

Likewise, there is a corresponding decrement operator.

counter--

is equivalent to

counter = counter – 1.

It is much easier to write counter++ or counter -- in the for-loop sentence.

There are also another set of shorthand operators called the generalized increment and decrement operators.

counter++ is equivalent to writing counter+=1
counter-- is equivalent to writing count-=1

Now the value to increment or decrement by does not need to be only 1. It can be any value.

```
counter += 2
counter += 3
```

and if counter was a real number, then the increment/decrement values could be real numbers also.

```
counter += 1.3
counter -= 5.67
```

In addition, the operators used need not be only + or -. It can also be multiply (*) and divide (/)

```
counter *= 2
counter /= 4
```

These operators are useful to know about as they are used frequently by programmers in expressions.

End of Diversion

Earlier I said there were three loop sentences. So far you have seen two of them, the while-loop sentence and the for-loop sentence. The third kind of loop is called the do-while sentence and it is shown below.

```
do
{
        ... code to repeat

} while (condition);
```

In this version of the loop-sentence the condition to test occurs at the end of the loop. This means that the body of the loop will always be executed at least once. Once again, consider what this loop would look like with our sample counting program.

```
counter = 0;
do
{
        counter++;
        cout << "Hello\n";
} while (counter < 10);
```

Why have three loops that basically do the same thing? Well in fact, they do not do the same thing.

The while-loop sentence and the do-while-loop sentence are usually used with a conditional sentence inside of the loop body. The conditional sentence can serve one of two purposes.

In one case, it is possible to cause a loop exit with a conditional sentence, and in the other case it is possible to skip part of the code inside the loop with a conditional sentence. Let's take a look at both of these cases.

In the Tic-Tac-Toe game, we would want to end the game when the player or the opponent has won the game. We could accomplish this with the following code.

```
while (true)
{
        ... Tic-Tac-Toe code

        if (playerWins || opponentWins) break;

        ... Rest of Tic-Tac-Toe code
}
```

The condition of the while-sentence is true, which means this loop will go on forever unless stopped somehow. Inside of the loop, the condition that stops the loop (exits the loop) is when the player wins or opponent wins the game. The special sentence "break" causes the loop to be exited with the program picking up at the statement after the loop body. Otherwise the game continues with the code after the if-sentence.

Another situation that will arise in the Tic-Tac-Toe game is when we learn that one of the players has won the game. There is no reason to execute the other player's code – we can skip it.

Let's suppose that the program checks to see if the player has won. Then we do not need to execute the code for the opponent. We can accomplish this with the following code.

```
while (true)
{
        ... Tic-Tac-Toe code

        if (playerWins) continue;

        ... Rest of Tic-Tac-Toe code to allow the opponent to
        move
}
```

In this case, the continue sentence causes the program to "jump" to the end of the loop and then begin the loop again.

Loop Exercises

For each of the following, write the loop-sentence as specified.

1) Write a for-loop sentence that counts from 1 to 100 in increments of 1.
2) Write a for-loop sentence that counts from 1 to 100 in increments of 10.
3) Write a for-loop sentence that counts backwards from 10*3.14 to 1*3.14 by increments of 3.14.
4) Write a while loop that ends when the variable end-of-loop becomes true.
5) Consider a container that will hold 3.4 gallons of water. The container is filled approximately .1 gallons each minute. Write a loop that will fill the container with water and stop when the container if filled with 3.4 gallons of water.
6) Write a loop that will read 15 values and compute the sum of these values.
7) Write a loop that will read values until a value of 999 is input by the user.

Let's continue with the Tic-Tac-Toe example we began earlier.

As a program Tic-Tac-Toe is more difficult then what you've seen so far. In the earlier discussion we used Tic-Tac-Toe to show some examples of if-sentences. Now we will tackle the whole program. There are still some things that you can learn to make a simpler program for the game. For now, though we will stick with what we know.

Whenever we write a program, we try to think about the program as a series of steps or parts. In the Tic-Tac-Toe game, one person usually takes the first move and the other person usually takes the next move and so on. In our case since the computer will be the opponent, it will always be the computer that takes the second move of each pair of moves. The following outline describes the steps of the game.

1) Game welcome
2) Game instructions
3) Repeat the following steps until there is a winner or until the game is tied
    a. The player takes a move
    b. The computer makes sure the move is a valid move
    c. The computer checks to see if the player has won
    d. If the player has won, skip the rest of the body of the loop because the game is over
    e. If the game is a tie, skip the rest of the body of the loop because the game is over
    f. The computer takes a move
    g. The computer checks to see if the opponent has won
    h. If the opponent has won the skip the rest of the body of the loop because the game is over
    i. If the game is a tie, skip the rest of the body of the loop because the game is over
4) Announce the winner of the game

This outline represents the steps of the game and also the steps of the program that will implement the game. This step-by-step outline is called an **algorithm**. Algorithms are very important to computer scientists. The fundamental job of the computer scientist is to write algorithms (and show that they do what they are supposed to do),

In step 1, we welcome the player to the game and in step 2 we tell the player what to do in order to take a move in the game.

Step 1) Welcome and
Step 2) Instructions

Output: Welcome to the game of Tic-Tac-Toe. You will be playing against the computer. You will take the first move in the game. To take a move you will select a cell in which to move. Cells are numbered from 1 to 9, from the top left, to the bottom right, as shown in the diagram below.

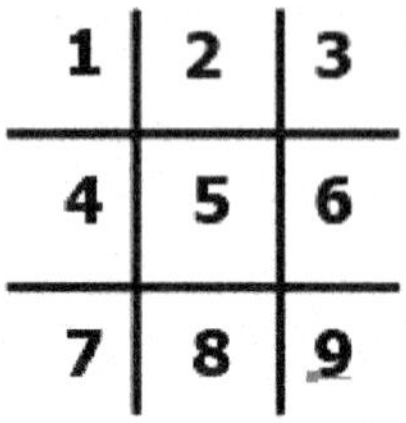

1	2	3
4	5	6
7	8	9

You can only select a cell in which to move if the cell has not already been selected. Once you select your move the computer will check your move to see if you won the game or tied the game. If the game is won or tied, the game is over and the winner of tie will be announced. Otherwise the opponent will select their move. In this case the opponent is the computer.

Of course the greeting and the instructions will be displayed as a series of cout statements as follows.

```
cout << "Welcome to the game of Tic-Tac-Toe.\n";
cout << "You will be playing against the computer. You will\n";
cout << " take the first move in the game. To take a move you\n";
cout << "will select a cell in which to move.
cout << "Cells are numbered\n";from 1 to 9, from the top left,\n";
cout << " to the bottom right, as shown in the diagram below.\n";
cout << "Facsimile of board here \n";
cout << "You can only select a cell in which to move if the\n";
cout << "cell has not already been selected. Once you select your\n";
cout << "move the computer will check your move to see if you\n".\;
cout << "won; the game or tied the game. If the game is won or\n";
cout << "tied, the game is over and the winner of tie will be\n";
cout << "announced. Otherwise the opponent will select\n";
cout << their move. In this case the opponent if the computer.\n";
```

At step 3 we begin a loop that will end when there is a winner or when there is a tie.

```
bool isPlayerWinner = false;     // set to true when there is a winner
bool isOpponentWinner = false;
bool isTie = false;              // set to true when there is a tie

do
{









} while (!(isPlayerWinner || isOppenentWinner || isTie));
```

At Step 3a, the player takes a move. He or she does so by selecting the location of where he or she would like to move.

```
bool isPlayerWinner = false;     // set to true when the player wins
bool isOpponentWinner = false; // set to true when the opponent wins
bool isTie = false;              // set to true when there is a tie
int playersMove = 0;
int opponentsMove = 0;
bool badMove = true;      // Assume badmove is true. Let the
                          // program verify that in fact the move
                          // is a good one
int topLeftOccupied = 0;         // is not zero when this cell is selected
int topCenterOccupied = 0;       // is not zero when this cell is selected
int topRightOccupied = 0;                // is not zero when this cell is selected
int centerLeftOccupied = 0;      // is not zero when this cell is selected
int centerCenterOccupied = 0; // is not zero when this cell is selected
int centerRightOccupied = 0;    // is not zero when this cell is selected
int bottomLeftOccupied = 0;     // is not zero when this cell is selected
```

```
int bottomCenterOccupied = 0;// is not zero when this cell is selected
int bottomRightOccupied = 0;  // is not zero when this cell is selected

do
{
```

Step 3a)

```
    cout << "Enter the number of the cell in which you would\n";
    cout << "like to move (0 if there is no place to move): ";
```

Step 3b)

```
    cin >> playersMove;

    // Make sure the number entered is between 1 and 9 and also make
    // sure the cell isn't taken


    while (true)  // We loop until the player has entered an
                  // acceptable move
    {
        if (playersMove < 0 || playersMove > 9)  badMove = true;

    // Now check each of the cells to see if the player selected an
    // occupied cell
```

Step 3e)

```
        if (playersMove == 0)
        {
            isTie = true;
            continue;
        }

        if  ((playersMove ==1) && topLeftOccupied != 0)
            badMove = true;
        if  ((playersMove ==2) && topCenterOccupied != 0)
            badMove = true;
        if  ((playersMove ==3) && topRightOccupied != 0)
            badMove = true;
        if  ((playersMove ==4) && centerLeftOccupied != 0)
            badMove = true
        if  ((playersMove ==5) && centerCenterOccupied != 0)
            badMove = true;
        if  ((playersMove ==6) && centerRightOccupied != 0)
```

```
            badMove = true;
    if ((playersMove ==7) && bottomLeftOccupied != 0)
            badMove = true;
    if ((playersMove ==8) && bottomCenterOccupied != 0)
            badMove = true;
    if ((playersMove ==9) && bottomRightOccupied !=0)
            badMove = true;

// If the player made a bad move then we need to ask the player to
// choose another move

    if (badMove)
    {
            cout << "The move you selected is invalid.\n";
            cout << "Please choose another cell in which to
                    move.\n";
            cin >> playersMove;
            badMove = false;
            continue;
    }

// Set the cell selected by the player as occupied by the player

    if (playerMove == 1) topLeftOccupied = 1
    if (playerMove == 2) topCenterOccupied = 1
    if (playerMove == 3) topRightOccupied = 1
    if (playerMove == 4) centerLeftOccupied = 1
    if (playerMove == 5) centerCenterOccupied = 1
    if (playerMove == 6) centerRightOccupied = 1
    if (playerMove == 7) bottomLeftOccupied = 1
    if (playerMove == 8) bottomCenterOccupied = 1
    if (playerMove == 9) bottomRightOccupied = 1

// See if the player is the winner of the game or if the game is
// now a tie

    isPlayerWinner = false;
    isTie = false;

// Look for a row of player occupied cells
```

Step 3d)

```
if (topLeftOccupied == 1 && topCenterOccupied == 1 &&
        topRightOccupied == 1) isPlayerWinner = true;
if (centerLeftOccupied == 1 && (centerCenterOccupied == 1
        && centerRightOccupied == 1) isPlayerWinner = true;
if (bottomLeftOccupied == 1 && bottomCenterOccupied
        == 1 && bottomRightOccupied == 1)
        isPlayerWinner = true;

// Look for a column of player occupied cells

if (topLeftOccupied == 1 && centerLeftOccupied == 1 &&
        bottomLeftOccupied == 1) isPlayerWinner = true;
if (topCenterOccupied == 1 && centerCenterOccupied
        == 1 && centerBottomOccupied == 1)
        isPlayerWinner = true;
if (topRightOccupied == 1 && centerRightOccupied == 1 &&
        bottomRightOccupied == 1) isPlayerWinner = true;

// Look for a diagonal of player occupied cells

if (topLeftOccupied == 1 && centerCenterOccupied == 1 &&
        bottomRightOccupied == 1) isPlayerWinner = true;
if (topRightOccupied == 1 && centerCenterOccupied
== 1 &&bottomLeftOccupied == 1) isPlayerWinner = true;

if (isPlayerWinner) continue;

// The opponent will move by choosing the first empty cell
// encountered
```

Step 3f)

```
opponentsMove = 0;

if (leftTopOccupied == 0)
{
        opponentsMove = 1;
        leftTopOccupid = -1;
}
else if (centerTopOccupied == 0)
```

```
{
        opponentsMove = 2;
        centerTopOccupid = -1;
}
else if (rightTopOccupied == 0)
{
        opponentsMove = 3;
        rightTopOccupid = -1;
}
else if (leftCenterOccupied == 0)
{
        opponentsMove = 4;
        leftCenterOccupid = -1;
}
else if (centerCenterOccupied == 0)
{
        opponentsMove = 5;
        centerCenterOccupid = -1;
}
else if (centerRightOccupied == 0)
{
        opponentsMove = 6;
        centerRightOccupid = -1;
}
else if (bottomLeftOccupied == 0)
{
        opponentsMove = 7;
        bottomLeftOccupid = -1;
}
else if (bottomCenterOccupied == 0)
{
        opponentsMove = 8;
        bottomCenterOccupid = -1;
}
else if (bottomRightOccupied == 0)
{
        opponentsMove = 9;
        bottomRightOccupid = -1;
}
```

```
        // Check to see if the opponent won

        // Look for a row of opponent occupied cells

Step 3g)        if (topLeftOccupied == -1 && topCenterOccupied == -1 &&
                    topRightOccupied == -1) isOpponentWinner = true;
                if (centerLeftOccupied == -1 && (centerCenterOccupied == 1
                    && centerRightOccupied == -1) isOpponentWinner
                    = true;
                if (bottomLeftOccupied == -1 && bottomCenterOccupied
                    == -1  && bottomRightOccupied == -1)
                    isOpponentWinner = true;

        // Look for a column of opponent occupied cells

                if (topLeftOccupied == -1 && centerLeftOccupied == -1 &&
                    bottomLeftOccupied == -1) isOpponentWinner = true;
                if (topCenterOccupied == -1 && centerCenterOccupied
                    == -1 && centerBottomOccupied == 1)
                    isOpponentWinner = true;
                if (topRightOccupied == -1 && centerRightOccupied == -1
                    && bottomRightOccupied == -1) isOpponentWinner
                    = true;

        // Look for a diagonal of opponent occupied cells

                if (topLeftOccupied == -1 && centerCenterOccupied == -1
                    && bottomRightOccupied == -1) isOpponentWinner =
                true;
                if (topRightOccupied == -1 && centerCenterOccupied
                == -1 &&bottomLeftOccupied == -1) isOpponentWinner
                = true;

Step 3h)} while (!(isOpponentWinner || isPlayerWinner || isTie));
Step 3i)
```

After looking at all of this you may decide that programming is not for you. In reality though you are seeing how important it is not to assume that computers know anything other than what they are programmed. Each and every possibility in the game has to be accounted for and there are still a couple of things we have not accounted for. The first of these is that we never display the Tic-Tac-Toe board as it develops. This would be extremely useful. And of course at the end of the game we did not say anything about who won or if the game was a tie. An important detail to say the least.

Let's now consider how this program works. We have written the program as one large block of code. Later on we will see how to break code like this into smaller pieces, but for now it is a good lesson to work with such a large block of code.

At the beginning of this code the program will display some text that explains how this game works. This is simply a display of some text that occurs as a result of a series of couts. After the couts is where the fun begins. The first thing that we do is to declare and initialize some variables. We will make a table of these variables so that we can keep track of the values of the variables.

isPlayerWinner	isOpponentWinner	isTie	playersMove	opponentsMove	badMove
false	false	false	0	0	true

In addition to these variables we have variables to keep track if a cell is occupied and what it is occupied by. There are nine such variables in all. The cells are labeled first from the top leftmost cell down to the bottom rightmost cell.

topLeftOccupied	topCenterOccupied	topRightOccupied
0	0	0

centerLeftOccupied	centerCenterOccupied	centerRightOccupied
0	0	0

bottomLeftOccupied	bottomCenterOccupied	bottomRightOccupied
0	0	0

There variables are defined to specifically keep track of whether or not a cell is occupied and what it is occupied by. If the cell is unoccupied, its value is 0. If the cell is a player's cell (occupied by an X) then the cell will be assigned a value of 1. Finally if the cell is an opponents cell (occupied by an O) then the cell will be assigned a -1. Given these values, how would you set the variables for the following TIcTacToe board?

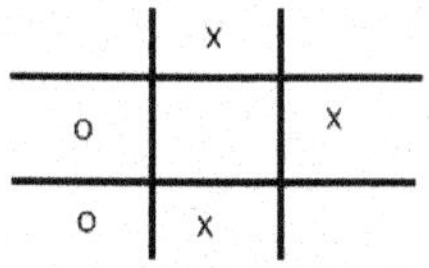

	X	
O		X
O	X	

topLeftOccupied	topCenterOccupied	topRightOccupied
0	1	0

centerLeftOccupied	centerCenterOccupied	centerRightOccupied
-1	0	1

bottomLeftOccupied	bottomCenterOccupied	bottomRightOccupied
-1	1	0

The variables would be set as shown above for the sample TicTacToe board.

As mentioned, at the start of the program a series of instructions will be displayed. These instructions tell the user how to play this game.

```
Welcome to the game of Tic-Tac-Toe
You will be playing against the computer. You will
You will take the first move in the game. To take a move
you will select a cell in which to place your mark.
Cells are numbered from 1 to 9, from the top left.
to the bottom right, as shown in the diagram below.


 1 | 2 | 3
==========
 4 | 5 | 6
==========
 7 | 8 | 9


You can only accept a cell to move if the
cell has not already been selected. Once you select your move
the computer will check your move to see if you made a valid
move, won the game, or tied the game. If the game is won or tied
computer will output a message and the game will end. Otherwise,
your opponent will make their move.
```

After the instructions have been displayed, the variables used by the program will be declared and initialized.

isPlayerWinner	isOpponentWinner	isTie	playersMove	opponentsMove	badMove
false	false	False	0	0	true

topLeftOccupied	topCenterOccupied	topRightOccupied
0	0	0

centerLeftOccupied	centerCenterOccupied	centerRightOccupied
0	0	0

bottomLeftOccupied	bottomCenterOccupied	bottomRightOccupied
0	0	0

A set of single character variables will also be initialized. These will hold the actual mark that is placed on the board of play.

topLeftSymbol	topCenterSymbol	topRightSymbol

centerLeftOccupied	centerCenterOccupied	centerRightOccupied

bottomLeftOccupied	bottomCenterOccupied	bottomRightOccupied

The next line of code begins the do {…} while (…) loop.

do {

// The user is prompted to enter a move by selecting one of the board cells.

```
Enter the number of the cell in which you would like to move.
Enter 0 if there is no cell available for you to move:
```

// to which the user enters a 5

```
Enter the number of the cell in which you would like to move.
Enter 0 if there is no cell available for you to move:
5
```

// The variable playersMove will contain the value 5.

isPlayerWinner	isOpponentWinner	isTie	playersMove	opponentsMove	badMove
false	False	false	5	0	true

// Next we check to see if playersMove is zero. If so it means there are no more moves for the player and the game should be ended. Since no one has won yet, it is assumed that the game is a tie.

// The game is not a tie in this case so the next thing that happens is we will check
// to see if the the value entered is a board cell that is already occupied.

centerLeftOccupied	centerCenterOccupied	centerRightOccupied
0	0	0

It is not occupied, so the move is okay.

```
badMove = false;

while (true) // loop until the player enters a correct cell selection
{
    if ((playersMove < 0) || (playersMove > 9)) badMove = true;

    if ((playersMove == 1) && topLeftOccupied != 0) badMove = true;
    if ((playersMove == 2) && topCenterOccupied != 0) badMove = true;
    if ((playersMove == 3) && topRightOccupied != 0) badMove = true;
    if ((playersMove == 4) && centerLeftOccupied != 0) badMove = true;
    if ((playersMove == 5) && centerCenterOccupied != 0) badMove = true;
    if ((playersMove == 6) && centerRightOccupied != 0) badMove = true;
    if ((playersMove == 7) && bottomLeftOccupied != 0) badMove = true;
    if ((playersMove == 8) && bottomCenterOccupied != 0) badMove = true;
    if ((playersMove == 9) && bottomRightOccupied != 0) badMove = true;
```

// At the top of the validation loop, badMove is set to false.

isPlayerWinner	isOpponentWinner	isTie	playersMove	opponentsMove	badMove
false	false	false	5	0	False

// badMove is not set – so the move is a valid one and we exit the loop.

```
        if (badMove)
        {
            cout << "The move you make is not valid" << endl;
            cout << "Please choose another move: ";
            cin >> playersMove;
            badMove = false;
            continue;
        }

        badMove = false;
        break;
    }

} while (...)
```

```
// Set the cell that is selected by the player as occupied by the player

if (playersMove == 1)topLeftOccupied = 1;
if (playersMove == 2)topCenterOccupied = 1;
if (playersMove == 3)topRightOccupied = 1;
if (playersMove == 4)centerLeftOccupied= 1;
if (playersMove == 5)centerCenterOccupied = 1;
if (playersMove == 6)centerRightOccupied = 1;
if (playersMove == 7)bottomLeftOccupied = 1;
if (playersMove == 8)bottomCenterOccupied = 1;
if (playersMove == 9)bottomRightOccupied = 1;
```

// Since the move is valid, we set the variable that tracks the state of a cell is set to
// 1 to indicate the cell is occupied by an x.

centerLeftOccupied	**centerCenterOccupied**	**centerRightOccupied**
0	1	0

// Once the move is recorded, we output an updated version of the game board
// with the new mark. This happens by way of the following if-sentences.
// The if-sentences place the mark

```
topLeftSymbol = ' ';
if (topLeftOccupied == 1) topLeftSymbol = 'X';
else if (topLeftOccupied == -1) topLeftSymbol = 'O';

topCenterSymbol = ' ';
if (topCenterOccupied == 1) topCenterSymbol = 'X';
else if (topCenterOccupied == -1) topCenterSymbol = 'O';

topRightSymbol = ' ';
if (topRightOccupied == 1) topRightSymbol = 'X';
else if (topRightOccupied == -1) topRightSymbol = 'O';

centerLeftSymbol = ' ';
if (centerLeftOccupied == 1) centerLeftSymbol = 'X';
else if (centerLeftOccupied == -1) centerLeftSymbol = 'O';

centerCenterSymbol = ' ';
if (centerCenterOccupied == 1) centerCenterSymbol = 'X';
else if (centerCenterOccupied == -1) centerCenterSymbol = 'O';

centerRightSymbol = ' ';
if (centerRightOccupied == 1) centerRightSymbol = 'X';
else if (centerRightOccupied == -1) centerRightSymbol = 'O';
```

```
bottomLeftSymbol = ' ';
if (bottomLeftOccupied == 1) bottomLeftSymbol = 'X';
else if (bottomLeftOccupied == -1) bottomLeftSymbol = 'O';

bottomCenterSymbol = ' ';
if (bottomCenterOccupied == 1) bottomCenterSymbol = 'X';
else if (bottomCenterOccupied == -1) bottomCenterSymbol = 'O';

bottomRightSymbol = ' ';
if (bottomRightOccupied == 1) bottomRightSymbol = 'X';
else if (bottomRightOccupied == -1) bottomRightSymbol = 'O';
```

And the set of cout statements outputs a printed version of the updated playing board.

```
cout << endl << endl;
cout << ' ' << topLeftSymbol << " | " << topCenterSymbol << " | " << topRightSymbol << endl;
cout << "===========" << endl;
cout << ' ' << centerLeftSymbol << " | " << centerCenterSymbol << " | " << centerRightSymbol << endl;
cout << "===========" << endl;
cout << ' ' << bottomLeftSymbol << " | " << bottomCenterSymbol << " | " << bottomRightSymbol << endl;
cout << endl << endl;
```

The updated board is displayed thusly.

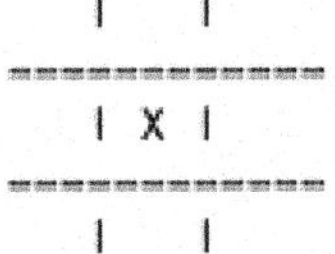

After a move is made, we check to see if the player has won. A series of if-sentences checks to see if a row contains the player's marks, if a column contains the player's marks, or if a diagonal contains the player's marks.

```
isPlayerWinner = false;
isTie = false;

// Look for a row of occupied cells

if (topLeftOccupied == 1 && topCenterOccupied == 1 && topRightOccupied == 1) isPlayerWinner = true;
if (centerLeftOccupied == 1 && centerCenterOccupied == 1 && centerRightOccupied == 1) isPlayerWinner = true;
if (bottomLeftOccupied == 1 && bottomCenterOccupied == 1 && bottomRightOccupied == 1) isPlayerWinner = true;

// Look for a column of occupied cells

if (topLeftOccupied == 1 && centerLeftOccupied == 1 && bottomLeftOccupied == 1) isPlayerWinner = true;
if (topCenterOccupied == 1 && centerCenterOccupied == 1 && bottomCenterOccupied == 1) isPlayerWinner = true;
if (topRightOccupied == 1 && centerRightOccupied == 1 && bottomRightOccupied == 1) isPlayerWinner = true;

// Look for a diagonal of occupied cells

if (topLeftOccupied == 1 && centerCenterOccupied == 1 && bottomRightOccupied == 1) isPlayerWinner = true;
if (bottomLeftOccupied == 1 && centerCenterOccupied == 1 && topRightOccupied == 1) isPlayerWinner = true;

if (isPlayerWinner) continue; // the play loop is now finished
```

None of these if-sentences are true so there is no winner yet.
The next step is for the opponent to make their move. The opponent in this version of the program is the computer. The strategy used by the computer is a simple one. The opponent moves to the first unoccupied cell.

In the next series of if-sentences, each cell is checked to see if it is occupied. The first unoccupied cell is chosen as the cell where the opponent will move.

```
opponentsMove = 0;

if (topLeftOccupied == 0)
{
    topLeftOccupied = -1;
    opponentsMove = 1;
}

else if (topCenterOccupied == 0)
{
    topCenterOccupied = -1;
    opponentsMove = 2;
}
else if (topRightOccupied == 0)
{
    topRightOccupied = -1;
    opponentsMove = 3;
}
else if (centerLeftOccupied == 0)
{
    centerLeftOccupied = -1;
    opponentsMove = 4;
}
else if (centerCenterOccupied == 0)
{
    centerCenterOccupied = -1;
    opponentsMove = 5;
}
else if (centerRightOccupied == 0)
{
    centerRightOccupied = -1;
    opponentsMove = 6;
}
else if (bottomLeftOccupied == 0)
{
    bottomLeftOccupied = -1;
    opponentsMove = 7;
}
else if (bottomCenterOccupied == 0)
{
    bottomCenterOccupied = -1;
    opponentsMove = 8;
}
else if (bottomRightOccupied == 0)
{
    bottomRightOccupied = -1;
    opponentsMove = 9;
}
```

In this case, the first cell that is unoccupied is cell #1. Once the cell is selected we display the updated game board with the opponent's move.

```
topLeftSymbol = ' ';
if (topLeftOccupied == 1) topLeftSymbol = 'X';
else if (topLeftOccupied == -1) topLeftSymbol = 'O';

topCenterSymbol = ' ';
if (topCenterOccupied == 1) topCenterSymbol = 'X';
else if (topCenterOccupied == -1) topCenterSymbol = 'O';

topRightSymbol = ' ';
if (topRightOccupied == 1) topRightSymbol = 'X';
else if (topRightOccupied == -1) topRightSymbol = 'O';

centerLeftSymbol = ' ';
if (centerLeftOccupied == 1) centerLeftSymbol = 'X';
else if (centerLeftOccupied == -1) centerLeftSymbol = 'O';

centerCenterSymbol = ' ';
if (centerCenterOccupied == 1) centerCenterSymbol = 'X';
else if (centerCenterOccupied == -1) centerCenterSymbol = 'O';

centerRightSymbol = ' ';
if (centerRightOccupied == 1) centerRightSymbol = 'X';
else if (centerRightOccupied == -1) centerRightSymbol = 'O';

bottomLeftSymbol = ' ';
if (bottomLeftOccupied == 1) bottomLeftSymbol = 'X';
else if (bottomLeftOccupied == -1) bottomLeftSymbol = 'O';

bottomCenterSymbol = ' ';
if (bottomCenterOccupied == 1) bottomCenterSymbol = 'X';
else if (bottomCenterOccupied == -1) bottomCenterSymbol = 'O';

bottomRightSymbol = ' ';
if (bottomRightOccupied == 1) bottomRightSymbol = 'X';
else if (bottomRightOccupied == -1) bottomRightSymbol = 'O';

cout << endl << endl;
cout << ' ' << topLeftSymbol << " | " << topCenterSymbol << " | " << topRightSymbol << endl;
cout << "===========" << endl;
cout << ' ' << centerLeftSymbol << " | " << centerCenterSymbol << " | " << centerRightSymbol << endl;
cout << "===========" << endl;
cout << ' ' << bottomLeftSymbol << " | " << bottomCenterSymbol << " | " << bottomRightSymbol << endl;
cout << endl << endl;
```

```
 O |   |
===========
   | X |
===========
   |   |
```

Let's fast forward to the point of the game where the player chooses the winning move. Here is the configuration of the game board at the point where the player can win. It is the player's move.

```
 O | X | O
===========
   | X |
===========
   |   |
```

Here the player should move in the bottom center cell, #8. This would allow the player to win in the vertical center row.

```
Enter the number of the cell in which you would like to move.
Enter 0 if there is no cell available for you to move:
```

We are prompted for a move and the player will enter 8.

```
Enter the number of the cell in which you would like to move.
Enter 0 if there is no cell available for you to move:
8


 O | X | O
-----------
   | X |
-----------
   | X |

The player has won the game.
Goodbye, come again.
```

The player enters an 8, and as expected wins the game with the center vertical column showing all X's.

In the program we verify that the move is valid and then set the value of the cell 8 to one. The cell variables look as shown below.

topLeftOccupied	topCenterOccupied	topRightOccupied
-1	1	-1

centerLeftOccupied	centerCenterOccupied	centerRightOccupied
0	1	0

bottomLeftOccupied	bottomCenterOccupied	bottomRightOccupied
0	0	0

topLeftSymbol	topCenterSymbol	topRightSymbol
O	X	O

centerLeftSymbol	centerCenterSymbol	centerRightSymbol
	X	

bottomLeftSymbol	bottomCenterSymbol	bottomRightSymbol

When the player enters 8 for their selection, the variables change as follows.

topLeftOccupied	topCenterOccupied	topRightOccupied
-1	1	-1

centerLeftOccupied	centerCenterOccupied	centerRightOccupied
0	1	0

bottomLeftOccupied	bottomCenterOccupied	bottomRightOccupied
0	1	0

topLeftSymbol	topCenterSymbol	topRightSymbol
O	X	O

centerLeftSymbol	centerCenterSymbol	centerRightSymbol
	X	

bottomLeftSymbol	bottomCenterSymbol	bottomRightSymbol
	X	

The next relevant part of the code is where the rows, columns, and diagonals are checked to see if there is a winner.

```
isPlayerWinner = false;
isTie = false;

// Look for a row of occupied cells
```

```
if (topLeftOccupied == 1 && topCenterOccupied == 1 && topRightOccupied == 1) isPlayerWinner = true;
if (centerLeftOccupied == 1 && centerCenterOccupied == 1 && centerRightOccupied == 1) isPlayerWinner = true;
if (bottomLeftOccupied == 1 && bottomCenterOccupied == 1 && bottomRightOccupied == 1) isPlayerWinner = true;

// Look for a column of occupied cells
```

B

```
if (topLeftOccupied == 1 && centerLeftOccupied == 1 && bottomLeftOccupied == 1) isPlayerWinner = true;
if (topCenterOccupied == 1 && centerCenterOccupied == 1 && bottomCenterOccupied == 1) isPlayerWinner = true;
if (topRightOccupied == 1 && centerRightOccupied == 1 && bottomRightOccupied == 1) isPlayerWinner = true;

// Look for a diagonal of occupied cells
```

C

```
if (topLeftOccupied == 1 && centerCenterOccupied == 1 && bottomRightOccupied == 1) isPlayerWinner = true;
if (bottomLeftOccupied == 1 && centerCenterOccupied == 1 && topRightOccupied == 1) isPlayerWinner = true;

if (isPlayerWinner) continue; // the play loop is now finished
```

Section A's if-sentences are not relevant because there is no row consisting of all X's. Likewise, section C's if-sentences do not apply to the situation. But the story for section B is different.

```
if (topLeftOccupied == 1 && centerLeftOccupied == 1 && bottomLeftOccupied == 1) isPlayerWinner = true;
if (topCenterOccupied == 1 && centerCenterOccupied == 1 && bottomCenterOccupied == 1) isPlayerWinner = true;
if (topRightOccupied == 1 && centerRightOccupied == 1 && bottomRightOccupied == 1) isPlayerWinner = true;
```

The first if-sentence checks the left-hand column. There are no left-hand column cells that have an X-value. The third if-sentence checks the right-hand column. Again there are no cells that have an X-value. But the center column is a different story.

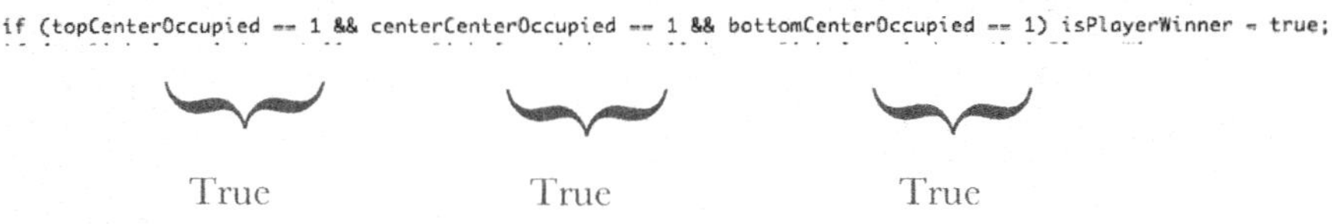

Since all three conditions are evaluated to a true value, the player has won and so isPlayerWinner is set to true. Once isPlayerWinner is true all of the sentences between the test of isPlayerWinner are skipped and we end up at the bottom or end of the loop.

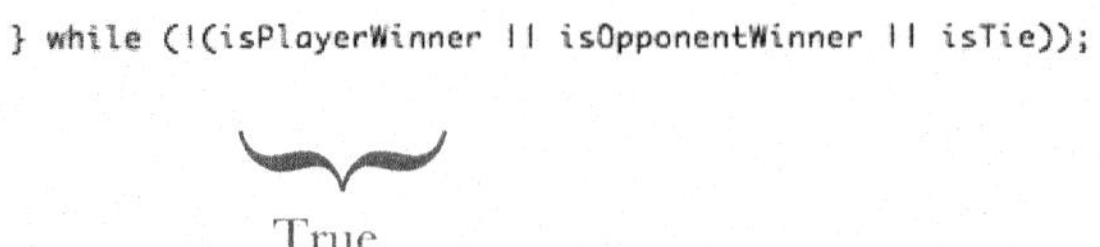

The loop will only continue if all three of the variables are false. Otherwise, the loop is exited, and the next three if-sentences determine the winner of the game.

```
if (isPlayerWinner) cout << "The player has won the game." << endl << "Goodbye, come again." << endl << endl;
if (isOpponentWinner) cout << "The opponent has won the game." << endl << endl;
if (isTie) cout << "The game is a tie." << endl << endl;
```

isPlayerWinner is true so we output a statement indicating that the player has won the game.

As you can see, when executing a complex program like this one, there are many steps to follow. In fact we are not finished our execution of this program because there are many other pathways that can be taken. As one does this, one gets more familiar with the program and may skip over the program sentences if they know the sentences will not be executed. In the beginning though, all sentences that are executed should be examined so the programmer understands what is happening in each sentence.

Chapter Exercise

1) To gain more experience with executing a program by hand, trace the program when the result will be a tie between the player and the opponent.

2) Change the program so that the player does not have to enter 0 when the game is over. In other words, get the program to figure out when the game is over.

3) Change the strategy that computer uses to select its move.

Chapter 8
One Variable/Many Memory Locations

Introduction to Arrays

You may have noticed in the Tic-Tac-Toe game that there are quite a few variables being used to represent the board. Fortunately, Tic-Tac-Toe is a relatively simple game, having only nine spaces on the board that must be represented. Consider a game like Chess that has 32 individual playing pieces to represent. Or a game of solitaire which has 52 different cards to represent. These games offer more of a challenge. In fact, most games would require a better way to represent the games to enable the computer to play them.

In this chapter we shall rewrite the TicTacToe game using a different representation for the game.

Every variable that we introduced can only be assigned a single value. Whenever that value is changed the previous value is lost. We say that it is overwritten by the new value. Every memory location can only hold a single value. This means that if we want to represent several different things we will need several different variables as we have seen. An array is a way around this problem. Different variables must have different names. One name per variable. In the case of an array, multiple variables can be accessed with a single name. This is magic !!

An array is a group of memory locations that can be accessed with one name. That name provides a reference in memory as to where the multiple values begin. It is the location of the beginning of the array.

Let's suppose that memory consists of these things called cells. Each cell can hold a value. Of course like any other variable, a cell must have a date type. You already know some of these, int, float, real, and char. So a cell must be given a type much as a variable is given a type. Actually, an array variable is just another kind of variable. The only difference is that the array variable refers to many values or as we have said cells.

In order that a single variable name can refer to more than one cell, an addressing scheme is used. Each cell has an address. Addresses begin at 0 and end at one less than the number of cells assigned to the array. Just as variables are declared, so are arrays. In fact the declaration sentence is very similar to the individual valued variable.

To declare an array of 10 integer elements we would write the sentence:

int arrayTen[10];

This creates an array of 10 elements. The address of the first element is at address 0 and the address of the last element is 9. If you were to draw a picture of the array it would look as shown below.

arrayTen

0	1	2	3	4	5	6	7	8	9

In this figure, the cells are labeled with their addresses which should not be confused with their values.

Storing a value in an array like arrayTen is similar to assigning a value to a variable. The assignment operator is used in the sentence. The left hand side of the assignment operator designates the cell of the array in which to store a value. The right hand side of the assignment operator contains an expression whose value will be stored.

Example 1)

arrayTen[5] = 12*3;

The array element would change as shown below.

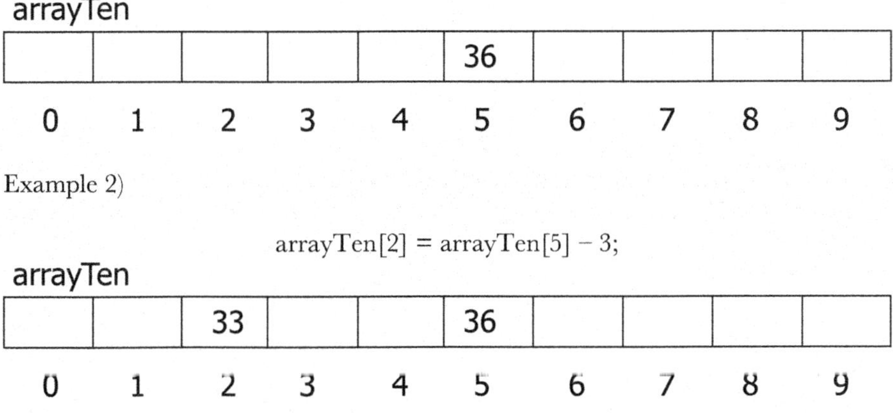

Example 2)

arrayTen[2] = arrayTen[5] – 3;

Example 3)

```
arrayTen[5] = 0;
```

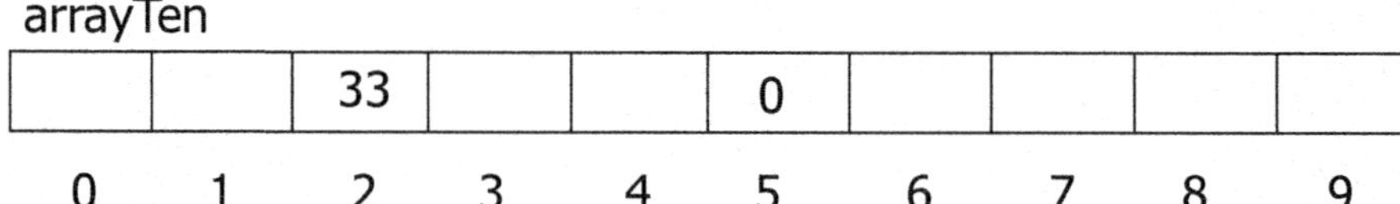

Just as in the case of a single value variable, the value of an individual array cell can be overwritten.

One of the advantages of using an array is its ability to have one name reference multiple values. By changing the array address an individual value in the array can be accessed with its address. The following code initializes all of the cells of the array using a loop.

```
for (int i=0; i<10; i++)
        arrayTen[i] = i;
```

When this code is run, arrayTen will look as follows.

	arrayTen									
CONTENT	0	1	2	3	4	5	6	7	8	9
ADDRESS	0	1	2	3	4	5	6	7	8	9

This loop initializes each element of the tenArray.

There is a shorthand for initializing arrays also. Supposing you wish to initialize arrayTen above without using a loop, but at the time of declaration. You can do so with the statement:

```
int arrayTen[] = {0,1,2,3,4,5,6,7,8,9};
```

Short Exercise

1) What is the 3rd element of arrayTen?
2) What is the 10th element of arrayTen?

3) What is the element at index 3 of arrayTen?
4) What is the element at index 10 of arrayTen?
5) How do you change the element at index 7 with a 0 in arrayTen?

One way to look at an array is like an ordered list of elements. The order of the list is determined by the index of the element.

Arrays are particularly useful when you have a lot of data you wish to process in the same way. For example, the following C++ sentences multiplies each of the elements of arrayTen by 3.

```
for (int i=0; i<10; i++)
        arrayTen[i] = arrayTen[i] * 3;
```

(Question: What is another way to write the expression arrayTen[i] = arrayTen[i] * 3; ?)

You may also want to add all of the numbers in an array. This can be accomplished by the following sentences in C++.

```
(1) int sum = 0;
(2) for (int i=0; i<10; i++)
(3)       sum = sum + arrayTen[i];
```

(Question: What is another way to write the expression sum = sum + ArrayTen[i]; ?)

Supposing you wanted to trace this code to make sure you are understanding what it does. Let's set up a tracing table to do just that.

Step	**I**	**arrayTen[i]**	**sum**
1	0	0	0
2	1	1	1
3	2	2	3
4	3	3	6
5	4	4	10
6	5	5	15
7	6	6	21
8	7	7	28
9	8	8	36

Let's consider another typical problem that would arise if we were going to write a program that used a deck of playing cards. In this case we would require two arrays, one for the value of the card (a number from 1 through 13) and a second for the suit of the card, a number from 1 to 4. We could set this up with a couple of loops. Supposing the suit array contains 13 sequences of the numbers 1 through 4. The meaning of these numbers is as follows:

1 = Diamond
2 = Spade
3 = Club
4 = Heart

The thirteen cards of each sub-deck would simply be the numbers from 1 to 13. Let's write some C++ sentences that accomplishes this. To accomplish this we need to use some variables. We will use the array named cardValues to hold the value of each of the cards stored there. We will use the array named cardSuits to hold the suit of each of the cards stores in the suit's array.

We also need two counters. One of these counters will be called suitNo to denote the number of the suit we are presently processing and cardValue to denote the value of the card we are presently processing. When we are finished setting up the array it would look as follows.

Array Index	Suit Value	Card Value	Card Name (not part of table)
0	1	1	1 of diamonds
1	1	2	2 of diamonds
2	1	3	3 of diamonds
3	1	4	4 of diamonds
4	1	5	5 of diamonds
5	1	6	6 of diamonds
6	1	7	7 of diamonds
7	1	8	8 of diamonds
8	1	9	9 of diamonds
9	1	10	J of diamonds
10	1	11	Q of diamond
11	1	12	K of diamonds
12	1	13	A of diamonds

A Note on the Side

Whenever you write a program, regardless of how simple or difficult you may find that you need it to do something that you don't know how to do. Back in the day, when this happened there were a couple of approaches to getting what you needed. The first was to ask a buddy how to do something. The second was to look it up (yuck, really ??). The third was to make up the code and hope it did what you wanted it to do. Nowadays we are blessed because we have the ultimate information source. I like to call it my "oracle" because with the proper keywords you can find code to do almost anything.

Anyway, the World Wide Web can be a tremendous learning resource. You can learn so much from what is out there provided you can separate the junk from the useful stuff. And in some cases you can learn how you can solve specific problems with code. There is nothing wrong with doing this. In fact most people who place code on the World Wide Web do so with that very idea. It is a good idea though to say where you got the code to give credit to the author. You can write this in the comments of your program. That way people know that you are using someone else's handiwork. Such is the case with what I am going to show you now.

There are two major types of games (actually many more). There are those games that are not random. They depend on a usually fixed set of rules and by using those rules you play the game with the hope that if you use them correctly and smartly you will eventually win the game. Chess is an example of such a game. The second major type of game depends on random chance. For example, all card games are of this type because the card you pick from the deck will be (or should be) unpredictable. Lots of times when we wish to write a game program of this type we want to be able to, for example, choose a random card. How can we do this? Let's say that we want a machine that will actually give us a random number each and every time we press a button on the front of the box. Here is one of those boxes in the next figure.

As you can see, for the most part, this is a black box. The reason is that we can't see how it works, but it does do what we want it to do. If we press the green button we will get a random number. Let's try it.

As you can see each time our friend presses the button to produce a random number, a new random number is produced. We don't know what is going on in the black box but it is doing what we want it to do. The point of this illustration is to show that we could have a mechanism that we don't understand and yet use that mechanism to our advantage. We actually do this all of the time. Consider, can you really explain how your game console works electronically. Probably not. The same principle holds here. We have some program code that does what we want it to and for the time being we don't have to understand it, we just have to be able to use it.

The code to produce a random number is:

r = rand() % 100;

The black box in this case is the special word rand(). rand() is called a function (there are many of these in C++), and its job is to produce a random number between 0 and 99. Here's an example of 10 random numbers produced by rand().

```
random number: 7
random number: 49
random number: 73
random number: 58
random number: 30
random number: 72
random number: 44
random number: 78
random number: 23
random number: 9
```

If we wanted to make sure that these numbers were between 1 and 100 we would use the following expression.

r = rand() % 100 + 1

We don't need numbers between 1 and 100 for our card deck. We need numbers between 1 and 13 and also 1 and 4 so we would use two different expressions.

r = rand() % 13 + 1
r = rand() % 4 + 1

Back from the Side

We will show you to how to get the computer to produce a shuffled card deck. By shuffled card deck we mean a deck whose cards are in a random order. That is the reason we had to show you how to make a random number.

The first step to produce the card deck is to create the arrays for the card deck. Remember that we are going to use two arrays. One for the value of the card and the second array for the suit of the card.

```
int deckSuits[52];
int deckFaces[52];
```

```
int randomPosition;
int randomCardSuit;
int randomCardFace;
int currentCardSuit;
int currentCardFace;

int cardIndex = 0;


for (int suitn = 1; suitn <= 4; suitn++)
      for (int facen = 1; facen <= 13; facen++)
      {
            deckSuits[cardIndex] = suitn;
            deckFaces[cardIndex] = facen;
            cardIndex++;
      }
```

What do we have after these code sentences are executed by the computer? Let' s carry out a partial trace of the code. We will need a column for the suitn index, facen index, the facen element of the deckSuits and the suitn element of the deckFaces array.

suitn	**Facen**	**deckSuits [facen]**	**deckFaces [suitn]**
1	1	1	1
1	2	1	2
1	3	1	3
1	4	1	4
1	5	1	5
... Until facen is 13 ...			
2	1	2	1
2	2	2	2
2	3	2	3
2	4	2	4
2	5	2	5
... Until facen is 13 ... ... Until suitn is 4 ...			

This is a partially filled in table of the deckSuits and deckFaces arrays. Once the deck is in the arrays in order, we can shuffle the decks and make them ready for play. This is where we can will use the random number sentences we showed earlier. The basic process is as follows.

> There are 52 cards in the deck and each card is in its ordinal place in the deck. We want to rearrange each card so that it is in a random place in the deck.

For each card in the deck -

1. Compute a random position in the deck
2. Move the current card in the deck to the position specified by the random position and move the card in the random position to the current position in the deck.

In code this looks something like as follows.

```
// Now randomize the cards in the deck

for (cardIndex = 0; cardIndex < 52; cardIndex++)
{
        randomPosition = rand() % 52;

        // Get the card in the randomly chosen position

                randomCardSuit = deckSuits[randomPosition];
                randomCardFace = deckFaces[randomPosition];

        // Get the card in the current position

                currentCardSuit = deckSuits[cardIndex];
                currentCardFace = deckFaces[cardIndex];

        // Swap the random card with the current card

                deckSuits[cardIndex] = randomCardSuit;
                deckFaces[cardIndex] = randomCardFace;
                deckSuits[randomPosition] = currentCardSuit;
                deckFaces[randomPosition] = currentCardFace'
}
```

As you can see from this code the first thing we do is to compute the random location of the current card. Then we save the current card and the card in the random location, and finally we swap the cards from their position. Here is the result of running this code (with a computer). You should try to hand simulate it as this will be great practice for you.

```
Card deck in order
Card #: 1 Suit 1 Face 1
Card #: 2 Suit 1 Face 2
Card #: 3 Suit 1 Face 3
Card #: 4 Suit 1 Face 4
Card #: 5 Suit 1 Face 5
Card #: 6 Suit 1 Face 6
Card #: 7 Suit 1 Face 7
Card #: 8 Suit 1 Face 8
Card #: 9 Suit 1 Face 9
Card #: 10 Suit 1 Face 10
Card #: 11 Suit 1 Face 11
Card #: 12 Suit 1 Face 12
Card #: 13 Suit 1 Face 13
Card #: 14 Suit 2 Face 1
Card #: 15 Suit 2 Face 2
Card #: 16 Suit 2 Face 3
Card #: 17 Suit 2 Face 4
Card #: 18 Suit 2 Face 5
Card #: 19 Suit 2 Face 6
Card #: 20 Suit 2 Face 7
Card #: 21 Suit 2 Face 8
Card #: 22 Suit 2 Face 9
Card #: 23 Suit 2 Face 10
Card #: 24 Suit 2 Face 11
Card #: 25 Suit 2 Face 12
Card #: 26 Suit 2 Face 13
Card #: 27 Suit 3 Face 1
Card #: 28 Suit 3 Face 2
Card #: 29 Suit 3 Face 3
Card #: 30 Suit 3 Face 4
Card #: 31 Suit 3 Face 5
Card #: 32 Suit 3 Face 6
Card #: 33 Suit 3 Face 7
Card #: 34 Suit 3 Face 8
Card #: 35 Suit 3 Face 9
Card #: 36 Suit 3 Face 10
Card #: 37 Suit 3 Face 11
Card #: 38 Suit 3 Face 12
Card #: 39 Suit 3 Face 13
Card #: 40 Suit 4 Face 1
Card #: 41 Suit 4 Face 2
Card #: 42 Suit 4 Face 3
Card #: 43 Suit 4 Face 4
Card #: 44 Suit 4 Face 5
Card #: 45 Suit 4 Face 6
Card #: 46 Suit 4 Face 7
Card #: 47 Suit 4 Face 8
Card #: 48 Suit 4 Face 9
Card #: 49 Suit 4 Face 10
Card #: 50 Suit 4 Face 11
Card #: 51 Suit 4 Face 12
Card #: 52 Suit 4 Face 13
```

```
Card deck randomized
Card #: 1 Suit 1 Face 12
Card #: 2 Suit 2 Face 5
Card #: 3 Suit 1 Face 6
Card #: 4 Suit 1 Face 11
Card #: 5 Suit 4 Face 4
Card #: 6 Suit 3 Face 10
Card #: 7 Suit 2 Face 8
Card #: 8 Suit 1 Face 5
Card #: 9 Suit 3 Face 6
Card #: 10 Suit 1 Face 10
Card #: 11 Suit 3 Face 11
Card #: 12 Suit 4 Face 2
Card #: 13 Suit 2 Face 6
Card #: 14 Suit 3 Face 2
Card #: 15 Suit 4 Face 9
Card #: 16 Suit 1 Face 4
Card #: 17 Suit 2 Face 4
Card #: 18 Suit 1 Face 2
Card #: 19 Suit 1 Face 13
Card #: 20 Suit 4 Face 6
Card #: 21 Suit 3 Face 3
Card #: 22 Suit 3 Face 5
Card #: 23 Suit 4 Face 10
Card #: 24 Suit 2 Face 9
Card #: 25 Suit 1 Face 3
Card #: 26 Suit 2 Face 10
Card #: 27 Suit 4 Face 11
Card #: 28 Suit 3 Face 13
Card #: 29 Suit 4 Face 8
Card #: 30 Suit 1 Face 1
Card #: 31 Suit 3 Face 4
Card #: 32 Suit 4 Face 7
Card #: 33 Suit 1 Face 9
Card #: 34 Suit 2 Face 3
Card #: 35 Suit 2 Face 1
Card #: 36 Suit 2 Face 12
Card #: 37 Suit 4 Face 1
Card #: 38 Suit 1 Face 7
Card #: 39 Suit 4 Face 12
Card #: 40 Suit 3 Face 1
Card #: 41 Suit 3 Face 8
Card #: 42 Suit 4 Face 5
Card #: 43 Suit 3 Face 12
Card #: 44 Suit 2 Face 2
Card #: 45 Suit 2 Face 11
Card #: 46 Suit 2 Face 7
Card #: 47 Suit 3 Face 7
Card #: 48 Suit 4 Face 3
Card #: 49 Suit 2 Face 13
Card #: 50 Suit 4 Face 13
Card #: 51 Suit 1 Face 8
Card #: 52 Suit 3 Face 9
```

If you check the randomized list of cards you will notice that each and every card in the ordered list is accounted for in the randomized list of cards.

Arrays So Far

In this chapter we have introduced the concept of arrays. An array is a variable name that can have multiple memory cells associated with it. In the Tic-Tac-Toe game we showed earlier, we had to use individual variables for each cell of the Tic-Tac-Toe board. Arrays are a way to avoid having to do this. We could have one variable named "board" and board can be used for all nine cells of the Tic-Tac-Toe board. We also showed that each element of an array has an address. The addresses begin at 0 and end at one less than the total number of elements in the array. For example, the card array of 52 elements has an initial element at address 0 and a final element at an address of 51 accounting for all 52 elements.

The arrays we have shown are called 1-dimensional arrays because each element has a single address. Although it is possible for an array to have as many elements as needed, it is also possible to have an array that has more than a single dimension.

Two-Dimensional Arrays

You can think of a 1-dimensional array as being like a single row of elements, each element numbered in sequential order. You can also envision a 1-dimensional array as a single column of elements. Sometimes it is useful to have an array that is more like a table consisting of rows and columns. Unlike a one dimensional array where each element has a single address (its position in the array), a 2-dimensional array, has two addresses. One of these addresses designates the row of the element and the other designates the column of the element. As in the case of the 1-dimemsional array, the top leftmost element of the 2-dimensional array is at row 0 and column 0. The remainder of the elements are numbered sequentially from left to right of each row and then down to the next row. A 3x3 2-dimensional array would be numbered as follows.

```
0,0|0,1|0,2
---------------
1,0|1,1|1,2
---------------
2,0|2,1|2,2
```

Sample 3x3 Array

A 2-dimensional array is declared by specifying both dimensions of the array. In the case of this example, we could declare it in the following way.

```
int example[3][3];
```

Accessing an element in a 2-dimensional array is similar to accessing an element in a 1-dimensional array. You access an element by specifying the element's address which in a 2-dimensional array consists of the row and columns of the element. For example, to access the element in the third row, and the second element of the row, we would use the indices [2] and [1].

```
0  |0  |0
---------------
0  |0  |0
---------------
0  |X  |0
```

example[2][1] = X

As I mentioned, it is possible to use a 2-dimensional array to represent a game board, like a Tic-Tac-Toe board. One of the other uses for it is to make a dot illustration with the arrays as the container for it. Consider the figure below.

```
        *
       . .
      . . .
     . * . . .
    . . . . . * .
   . . . . . . . . .
  . . . . . . . . . . .
       . . . .
       . . . .
       . . . .
       . . . .
  . . . . . . . . . . .
  . . . . . . . . . . .
```

So here is a dot-picture of a Christmas tree. We can store this in an array and print this whenever we want to display a Christmas tree as part of the output of a program. The size of the 2-dimensional array required for this dot-picture is 13 rows and 20 column positions.

char dotPicture[13][20]

Code to create the dot-picture.

```
// Blank the array

for (int i=0; i<13; i++)
        for (int i=0; i<20; i++)
                dotPicture[i] = ' ';

// Set the tree points in the array

// Line 1
dotPicture[0,10] = '.';

// Line 2
dotPicture[1,9] - '.';
dotPicture[1,11] = '.';
```

```
// Line 3
dotPicture[2,8] = '.';
dotPicture[2,10] = '.';
dotPicture[2,12] = '.';

// Line 4
dotPicture[3,6] = '.';
dotPicture[3,8] = '*';
dotPicture[3,10] = '.';
dotPicture[3,12] = '.';
dotPicture[3,14] = '.';

// Line 5
dotPicture[4,4] = '.';
dotPicture[4,6] = '.';
dotPicture[4,8] = '.';
dotPicture[4,10] = '.';
dotPicture[4,12] = '.';
dotPicture[4,14] = '*';
dotPicture[4,16] = '.';

// Line 6
dotPicture[5,3] = '.';
dotPicture[5,5] = '.';
dotPicture[5,7] = '.';
dotPicture[5,9] = '.';
dotPicture[5,11] = '.';
dotPicture[5,13] = '.';
dotPicture[5,15] = '.';
dotPicture[5,17] = '.';

// Line 7
dotPicture[6,2] = '.';
dotPicture[6,4] = '.';
dotPicture[6,6] = '.';
dotPicture[6,8] = '.';
dotPicture[6,10] = '.';
dotPicture[6.12] = '.';
dotPicture[6,14] = '.';
dotPicture[6,16] = '.';
```

```
dotPicture[6,18] = '.';

// Line 8
dotPicture[7,8] = '.';
dotPicture[7,10] = '.';
dotPicture[7,12] = '.';
dotPicture[7,14] = '.';

// Line 9
dotPicture[8,8] = '.';
dotPicture[8,10] = '.';
dotPicture[8,12] = '.';
dotPicture[8,14] = '.';

// Line 10
dotPicture[9,8] = '.';
dotPicture[9,10] = '.';
dotPicture[9,12] = '.';
dotPicture[9,14] = '.';

// Line 11
dotPicture[10,8] = '.';
dotPicture[10,10] = '.';
dotPicture[10,12] = '.';
dotPicture[10,14] = '.';

// Line 12
dotPicture[11,2] = '.';
dotPicture[11,4] = '.';
dotPicture[11,6] = '.';
dotPicture[11,8] = '.';
dotPicture[11,10] = '.';
dotPicture[11,12] = '.';
dotPicture[11,14] = '.';
dotPicture[11,16] = '.';
dotPicture[11,18] = '.';

// Line 13
dotPicture[12,2] = '.';
dotPicture[12,4] = '.';
```

```
dotPicture[12,6] = '.';
dotPicture[12,8] = '.';
dotPicture[12,10] = '.';
dotPicture[12,12] = '.';
dotPicture[12,14] = '.';
dotPicture[12,16] = '.';
dotPicture[12,18] = '.';
```

And that is how you can use a 2-dimensional array to carry the data to draw a picture of a simple tree.

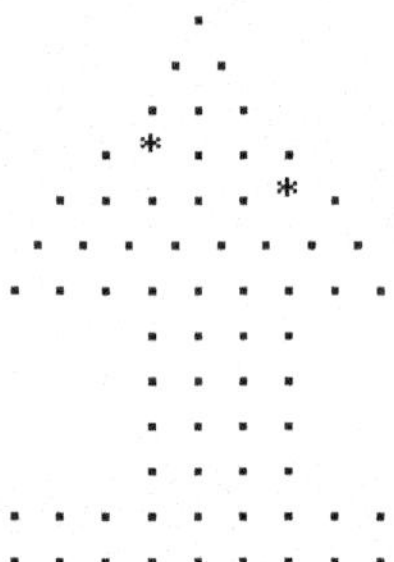

Chapter Exercises

Chapter Exercise 1

(Easy) In the Christmas Tree program there is a lot of repetition. Can you can this code so that there is a better was to accomplish this repetition – say without so many statements that are the same?

(Modertate) Can you change the Christmas Tree program to use arrays as opposed to individual statements?

Chapter Exercise 2

(Challenging) See if you can write a C++ program that will output a graphics as shown in the tree example above, that forms the shape of the 26 letters of the alphabet. In the program you write, allow the user to enter a letter and the program will respond by producing the graphics of that letter. If the character is entered is incorrect, tell the user and allow them to correct the letter. Keep going until the user enters the word END.

Chapter Exercise 3

(Extremely Challenging) See if you can modify the Tic-Tac-Toe game presented earlier to use a 2-dimensional array as opposed to individual variables.

Note: Remember you are not writing a program to run on the computer but you ARE writing a program you will execute using paper and pencil.

Section 8.1 Conditional Done Industrial Style

Courtesy: https://i.ytimg.com/vi/3eUs-l7Ss24/maxresdefault.jpg

In case you've never seen something like the construction shown in the photo above, this is called a train turntable. Its purpose is to take a train (engine and/or cars) and in an efficient way change the track on which that train is riding. Its overall operation is rather simple as you can see. The center portion of track turns to place the train on the desired track and then the train can ride into the train house for storage or repair or proceed along another track. If you think of this mechanism as a kind of mechanical if-sentence, the movement of the train to a different track (path) corresponds to taking a different track in a program through the use of an if-sentence.

In C++ this would be akin to writing a series of if-sentences that look something like the following. Supposing we have a variable named selection.

Selection will be set to an integer value. Usually selection will be an integer and range in value from 1 to some largest value – for example 10 as an arbitrary value.

```
if (selection == 1) ...      // go do something when selection has the value 1
if (selection == 2) ...      // go do something when selection has the value 2
if (selection == 3) ...      // go do something when selection has the value 3
if (selection == 4) ...      // go do something when selection has the value 4
if (selection == 5) ...      // go do something when selection has the value 5
if (selection == 6) ...      // go do something when selection has the value 6
if (selection == 7) ...      // go do something when selection has the value 7
if (selection == 8) ...      // go do something when selection has the value 8
if (selection == 9) ...      // go do something when selection has the value 9
if (selection == 10) ...     // go do something when selection has the value 10
```

These partial if-sentences should make some sense to you as they are similar to those we have shown earlier.

If we had 20 values of selection, we would have to write 20 if-sentences – one for each value. It would be nice if we had another way to accomplish the same activity but with something like the train turntable. In other words, if we knew the value of the selection variable then we would be able to choose the path of code to take in the program. There is such a sentence. It is called the switch-sentence. The sentence consists of several parts that could best be called clauses.

A switch-sentence begins with the word "switch." Following the word "switch" is an expression that, as usual is enclosed in parenthesis. The expression must evaluate to either an integer or a character value. In our case, the variable selection is an integer valued variable. (An integer type variable).

The clauses that make up the switch statement each have the same structure. Each clause begins with the word "case" and designates specific instructions for what to do when that value is encountered. Following the keyword "case" comes the value about which we want to perform some action. If the value is a 1, we would write,

case 1:

After the colon, you can place any executable statement. The last of these is a signal that there are no more clauses, a break sentence.

```
case 1:     do something when selection is 1;
            do the next thing when selection is 1;
            do still another thing when selection is 1;
            break;
```

A switch statement may have as many clauses as are needed to handle the various values of the selection variable. If, for example there are 10 selection values you may have 10 selection clauses. On the other hand, let's suppose that you want to do the same thing when the selection value is 1 and the selection value is 2. You can create two separate switch clauses for this purpose as in,

```
case 1:     do something when selection is 1;
            do the next thing when selection is 1;
            do still another thing when selection is 1;
            break;
case 2:     do something when selection is 2;
            do the next thing when selection is 2;
            do still another thing when selection is 2;
            break;
```

But since the thing that needs to be done when the selection value is 1 and the thing to be done when the selection value is a 2 are the same, we actually have something more like:

```
case 2:     do something when selection is 1 or 2;
            do the next thing when selection is 1 or 2;
            do still another thing when selection is 1 or 2;
            break;
```

which can be made into a single clause as follows:

```
case 1:
case 2:     do something when selection 1 or 2;
            do the next thing when selection is 1 or 2;
```

```
                do still another thing when selection is 1 or 2;
                break;
```

There may be a case when the value of the selection variable has no special processing associated with it, a special clause can be created for that situation. The special clause "default" is used for that purpose.

When there is no clause that applies to the selection variable it is a value for which there is no special processing for a value of the selection variable a default clause can be used. This is simply a clause that begins with they keyword default as in:

```
default:    do something for any other value of selection;
            do something else for any other value of selection;
            and so on ...
            break;
```

The default clause must also be the last clause of the switch sentence.

```
switch (selection)
{
        case 1:         ....
                        break;
        case 2:         ...
                        break;
        case 3:         ...
                        break;
        default:        ...
                        break;
}
```

It is important to remember that each switch clause must finish with a break; sentence. This is because if it does not, the switch statement will not know which statement to execute next.

What is the point of the "break" sentence in a switch sentence? (you may be wondering). Sometimes, in order to be able for a computer process a programming language it is necessary to make some allowances for what a computer can process and understand. These are called syntactic crutches. These are a means of helping the computer with a program that it might be difficult to understand otherwise. So this is one of the reasons that each of the break sentences must be included in a switch statement. Technically though there is a different and quite appropriate reason given.

If a break sentence is omitted from a clause of a switch statement then when the code is executed by the computer, when a break statement is not present, the computer will think that the rest of the code in the switch statement is actually part of the code of the case clause to be executed. We say that the code in the switch falls through to the the rest of the code in the switch statement which may not be (usually not) the intention of the programmer. Some examples may help to make this clearer.

Let's formulate a switch statement that is part of a calculator program. The switch statement helps the program "understand" what to do when a certain arithmetic operator is encountered. There will be a section of code to handle the situation when the operator is an addition sign, a subtraction sign, a multiplication sign, and a division sign. There are two variables defined in the program, op1 and op2 which are used to contain the left hand and right hand operands of the operators. Here is the switch sentence that I propose.

```
switch (operator)
{
        case '+':     result = op1 + op2;
                      break;
        case '-':     result = op1 – op2;
                      break;
        case '*':     result = op1 * op2;
                      break;
        case '/':     result = op1 / op2;
                      break;
        default:      cout << "The operator is incorrect."
                      << endl;
                      break;
}
```

This switch sentence should be fairly easy to understand. The first task I would ask you to is to demonstrate that you do understand what this statement does is to translate the switch-sentence into a series of if-sentences. If you do understand what this sentence does and also what if-sentences do understanding what the corresponding if-sentences do should not be a challenge for you.

Short Exercise

Write the if-sentences that carry out the same behavior as the switch-statement below. In the code that you write, use the return sentence in the same way that you would use the break statement. The correct code follows on the next page.

```
if (operator == '+')
{
        result = op1 + op2;
        return result;
}

if (operator == "-")
{
        result = op1 - op2;
        return result;
}

if (operator == '*')
{
        result = op1 * op2;
        return result;
}

if (operator == '/')
{
        result = op1 / op2;
        return result;
}

cout << "The operator is incorrect" << endl;
return -1;      // -1 indicates that there is no result from this code
```

Although this will be explained in detail later, consider that the return sentence accomplished the same task as the break sentence in the switch statement.

Now if we were to remove the first return sentence in the sequence of the if-sentences consider what would occur if the code for the addition operator was executed.

```
if (operator == '+')
{
        result = op1 + op2;
}

if (operator == "-")
{
        result = op1 - op2;
        return result;
}

if (operator == '*')
{
        result = op1 * op2;
        return result;
}

if (operator == '/')
{
        result = op1 / op2;
        return result;
}

cout << "The operator is incorrect" << endl;
return -1;    // -1 indicates that there is no result from this code
```

By removing the return statement, the next statement to be executed after result = opt1 + opt2 will be the next if-sentence

But in this case, it doesn't matter because the if-sentence will not allow the code within the if-sentence to be executed

On the other hand, if we remove the break-sentence in the corresponding switch statement we have a different result.

```
switch (operator)
{
        case '+':    result = op1 + op2;

        case '-':    result = op1 – op2;
                     break;
        case '*':    result = op1 * op2;
                     break;
        case '/':    result = op1 / op2;
                     break;
```

```
        default:    cout << "The operator is incorrect."
                    << endl;
                    break;
    }
```

As you can see, the next sentence that will be executed will be the sentence result = op1 – op2 because the break statement has been removed.

Chapter 9
The Function of Functions

We shall end our sojourn into thinking C++ Part 1 with a discussion of the extremely important concept of the function. In some senses, the function consists of two things as do all of the concepts so far introduced as part of the programming language C++. First, of course, there is the structure of the sentence – the way that the sentence defining a function is written. Second there is a purpose to the sentence. The purpose of the function is to organize the thoughts of a program. If we think of a program as an essay, then the function divides the programmatic essay into its component thoughts.

It is difficult to explain what a function is much as it was probably difficult to understand what a paragraph was in an English composition when you first learned about one. If you remember, a paragraph expresses one complete thought. If you were anything like me though this definition was confusing because doesn't a sentence express a complete thought also? Somehow, the teachers that I had thought this was an obvious concept. A paragraph expresses a complete thought while a sentence expresses ???? Something less than a thought. Maybe a sentence expresses a thought but it is not a full thought – it is only a part of a thought. Maybe a sentence expresses a mini-thought. A mini-thought is not a big thought as would be expressed in a paragraph but rather a thought that could only be part of a paragraph. A sentence couldn't stand on its own. I feel myself getting confused. This same confusion can be applied to programs also. It would seem a programing sentence represents a complete thought in a programming language but a programming paragraph, a function, also represents some kind of complete thought in the programming language. How could two concepts be the same thing? Ughh !

Just as a sentence is an expression of a thought, so too is a paragraph. The difference between the thought a sentence expresses and that which a paragraph expresses is a matter of scope. We can think of scope as a matter of coverage. The capability of a sentence to cover a thought is fundamental to a sentence. For example, a sentence about a ball rolling down a hill is entirely possible in a single sentence.

"A large red ball is rolling down the hill."

This is only a single thought as represented by this sentence. We may wish to express some additional information as part of this sentence. When the ball reaches the bottom of the hill, it is stopped by a rock at the bottom of the hill.

> "A large red ball is rolling down the hill where
> it is stopped by a rock at the bottom of the hill."

Once the ball is stopped at the bottom its forward momentum causes the ball to bounce backward a couple of feet.

> "A large red ball is rolling down the hill where
> it is stopped by a rock at the bottom of the hill and
> then bounces backwards for a couple of feet before it
> comes to rest."

This is still a single sentence expressing a thought about about a red ball. Granted, there are several parts to this sentence. This sentence represents a package of thoughts in the sense that it stands as a single unit. After a time though as parts are added to the sentence, the sentence becomes unwieldy or ceases to sound like a sentence and is much better when it is structured as a paragraph which is the next logical unit that we can use when writing. We want to say something about the red ball after is comes to rest.

> "A large red ball is rolling down the hill where
> it is stopped by a rock at the bottom of the hill and
> then bounces backwards for a couple of feet before it
> comes to rest. When the ball finally comes to rest, it
> begins to spin and as it spins changes colors more rapidly
> until the color blends into a uniform white color. When it
> becomes white it begins to bounce."

A paragraph is a group of sentences about a single thought that can be used to extend the content expressed by a sentence. It becomes somewhat tricky though to decide when to break to a new paragraph. The rule, "each paragraph expresses a new idea" is sometimes difficult to discern. Be that as it may the metaphor of sentence/paragraph, programming language statement/function is a good one to use as the basis of explaining a function and its purpose. A function is a unit of organization within a program.

So if you can extend this metaphor into our programming language knowledge thus far, the purpose of a function is to gather together two or more sentences in the language C++ and create a paragraph of sentences we call a function. Let's consider a very simple example of a function. In the following example look carefully because it shows the grouping of sentences in the C++ language but it also shows the structure it must take when written.

```
int addab (int a, int b)
{
        int sum;
        sum = a + b;
        return sum;
}
```

Before we get to how a function is assembled, let's see if you can answer a question about this function. What are the individual C++ statements in this function. See if you can circle each and don't worry about the sentences in this function that are specific to the function. For your convenience these have been highlighted in red so you can ignore them while answering the question.

```
int addab (int a, int b)
{
        int sum;
        sum = a + b;
        return sum;
}
```

Now consider what sentences are part of the basic sentences in the C++ language. Write them below.

```
(1)int addab (int a, int b)
(2){
(3)     int sum;
(4)     sum = a + b;
(5)     return sum;
(6)}
```

The two lines in yellow are ones that come from the sentences we learned that are part of the basic C++ language. This leaves sentences 1, 5 and punctuation 2, and 6.

Statement (1) is called a function header. Its purpose is to denote or define the beginning of a function. Every function written in C++ has a function header and soon you will see that there is a very special purpose for having such a sentence. The last sentence of note, sentence 5, is the return sentence. In order to understand what is happening with a return statement you must first understand what is happening in the call to the function. A function call is an activation of the code in the function. When we say that a function is called we are saying that we are calling upon the code of the function to be executed (or run). Right now the function as we have defined it is self-contained as it should be. If you were to just write the code of the function, nothing would happen in your program, at least related to the function. You might as well have not included it in your program. Of course we don't just write code in any program without having some purpose for it.

We say that a function is called when a reference is made to the function somewhere else in the program. This reference elsewhere in your program is nothing more than writing the function name. We call such a reference a call to the function. It tells the computer to execute the contents (and only the contents) of the function. In a function, when a return statement is encountered, it signals that the code in the function has been completed and the next code to be executed is the code that comes right after the call to the function. What happens looks similar to what is depicted in the next figure.

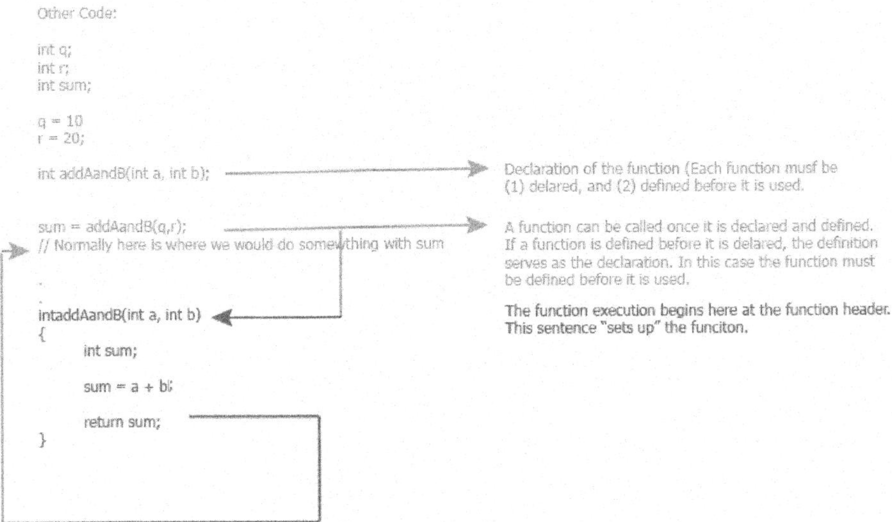

What you see in this figure are the basic mechanics of the function, its declaration, and its invocation. There is still an important part to be considered and that is how functions can take data into themselves and how functions can send data outward to the code that invokes the function.

Passing-IN AND Passing-OUT

Whenever we are sending data into a function we are saying that we are passing data into a function. In the other direction, we say that we are passing data out of a function. It is possible to pass as many data items (variables) into a function as you wish. Coming out of the function you can only pass one data item out of the function. Right now this might seem like a limitation but it is not as we shall see.

In the example above the function declaration (also called the function header) has several different parts.

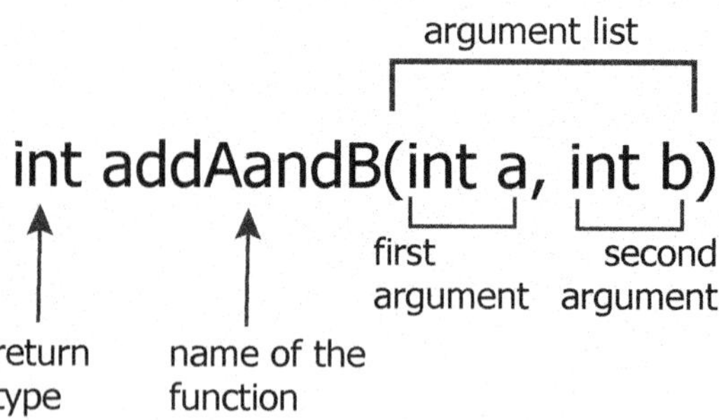

Within the argument list, each of the arguments, a portal through which data will pass has a data type and also a name. The arguments in this list are called "formal" in that they can represent any value of the type defined.

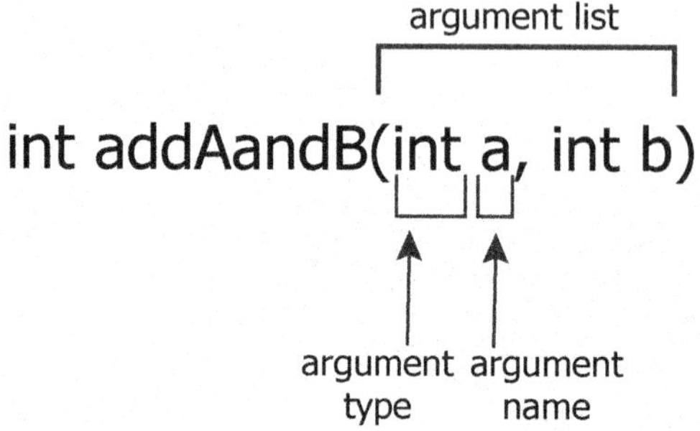

Let's suppose that I've written a program that uses this function. We shall define two variables q and r with both of these variables being of the integer type. We will allow the user to enter values for these variables.

```
(1) int q;
(2) int r;
(3) int sum;

(4) out << "Please specify the first variable: ";
(5) cin >> q;
(6) cout << "Please specify the second variable: ";
(7) cin >> r;
```

```
(8) sum = addAandB(q, r);
(9) cout << "The sum of A and B are: " << sum <<
    endl;


(1) int addAandB(int a, int b)
(2) {
(3) int sum;
(4) sum = a + b;
(5) return sum;
(6) }
```

When tracing a program that uses one or more functions it is a good idea to set up a table for each of the functions. This is because the variables that are passed from the calling program to the function may undergo a name change in the function. Usually we call the code that calls another function, the caller.

Name of the code: caller			
Statement #	q	r	Sum

Name of the code: addAandB			
Statement #	a	b	sum

In lines 5 and 7 let's assume that the user enters the values 15 and 7. That means that q = 15 and r = 7. The caller trace table becomes:

Name of the code: caller			
Statement #	q	r	Sum
5	15		
7		7	
8	Called addAandB		
8			22

Name of the code: addAandB			
Statement #	a	b	sum
1	15	7	
3			int
4			22
5			return 22

The arguments in for formal parameter list of the function act as doorways into the function. Each doorway allows one piece of data through it. When the data passes through the doorway it is renamed to the variable name used in the formal parameter list. This is why q becomes a and r becomes b in the simulation tables. These are one way doorways in that data can only move into the function through the doorway.

Notice in statement 8 of the caller code that the variable sum is set to the value of the function. This is because the function acts like a doorway also but instead of allowing data into the function, a value comes out of the function. This value is called the return value of the function and you can think of the function name as a sort of outlet that produces the result of the function.

At this stage of thinking about programming, a function is used as a means of breaking a program into smaller pieces. This is especially important when a program becomes large. When a function is defined that does a specific task it is easier to debug that function then if it was a self-contained bit of code as opposed to a bit of code embedded in a larger program. The smaller and more well-defined the function is, the easier it will be to debug

An important part of thinking about functions of a program is to consider the logical parts of the program. Consider the Tic-Tac-Toe program we presented earlier. We can see how that may be broken down into several smaller, special purpose functions. These smaller functions will be easier to understand and necessarily easier to debug.

In the Tic-Tac-Toe game, there were a sequence of activities that took place in order that the player is able to play the game. Let's recall those activities.

1) The game begins by displaying the title of the game and the the instructions for the game are displayed.
2) Display the playing board identifying each space on the board.
3) Start a playing loop
4) Ask the player for their move
5) Make sure the player's move is valid
    a. Check to see if the player has won the game
    b. Update board display
    c. if invalidMove()
        i. displaymessage()
        ii. return to step 4
6) If the player has won the game, end the game and announce the player has won
7) If there is no move for the computer to make,
    a. Game is a tie
    b. End the game
8) The computer chooses a move
    a. Update the board
    b. Display the board
9) If the computer won the game,
    a. announce that the computer has won the game

b. end the game.
10)Return to step 4

This breakdown of steps for the Tic-Tac-Toe game lends itself to a definition of set of functions that perform game play of Tic-Tac-Toe. Let's define a set of function headers that corresponds to this list of steps of the game.

Line numbers are included to make correspondence between English descriptions above and function headers below.

1) displayInstructions()
2) displayPlayingBoardLayout()
3) while (gameNotEnded)
4) {move = getPlayersMove()
5) validMove = validatePlayersMove(move)
    a. playerWins = checkifPlayerWins()
    b. updateBoard()
    c. displayBoard()
6) if (playerWins()) {... break ...}
7) if (noMove()) { ... break ...}
8) move = calculateComputerMove()
    a. updateBoard()
    b. displaBoard()
9) computerWins = checkifComputerWins(move)
    a. if (computerWins) {... break ...}
10)}

Exercise

(This exercise is very difficult)

Part 1 – See if you can write the rest of the program (i.e., fill in the blanks).
Part 2 – See if you can test the program by running the program using pencil and paper.

Chapter 10
Summary – Thinking C++

The goal of this book was twofold. First it was to show you the basic concepts of a programming language named C++. This language is called a programming language because it is used by computer to carry out the instructions you write in this language. You may have noticed that at no time while any information was conveyed in this book did you actually use a computer. Everything you had to do was either part of the book or using pencil and paper. You will see that this theme continues although in the second part of this series you will begin to use the computer in very specific ways.

The point is that before you can actually write programs for the computer you must know how to write programs for yourself. If you can't do the latter, the former will be impossible (or very difficult).

This book focuses with an introduction to the language C++ language by considering it as a language made up of words, sentences, and paragraphs. Although the analogy is by no means perfect it is meant to give you a way to remember and organize parts of the C++ language.

The focus of this book consisted of the basic C++ parts.

constants
types
variables
expressions
operators
assignment
conditionals
iteration
funcitons

In my conversations with others, there is a fairly strong belief that little can be done when writing a computer program without a computer. A computer is necessary to create and be able to see what the computer does when it runs your program. In other words it is a a necessary and sufficient condition that to be successful at programming that one must have a computer and that one must know how to use that computer to be able to see what a program does when it is written. It is a necessary and sufficient condition of programming in order to be successful at it. I am tempted to carry out a proof that actually contradicts this statement. The basic premise of contradiction would be to prove that a brain can simulate a computer. If the brain can simulate a computer then then either the necessity or sufficiency of needing a computer to carry out programming would be contradicted. The point I am trying to make is that if the equivalence is true then a mechanical or electronic computer is essentially equivalent to a biological computer (the brain).

The value of this claim is extremely important because it means that people will be able to learn how to program by using their brain to construct a program and use their brain as the means by which a programming is executed. If a human brain can execute a program, and if the result of the program is correct, one could expect that a computer would also run the program correctly. Therefore the original assumption underlying this book and those that will follow are correct. A person can learn to program a computer without a computer.

Appendix A
Punctuation and Vocabulary

Punctuati on Symbol	Punctuation Description
;	Semi-colon. Primarily used to indicate the end of a sentence in the C++ programming language. A semi-colon is like the period (.) in English that is typically used to end a sentence.
,	A comma is a separator character. Typically when you are writing a list of things, each item in that list will be separated from the next item with a comma as in the list a,b,c,d,e,f
{ } (Left and Right brace)	These symbols, the left and right brace are always used in a pair. The left brace, sometimes called the opening brace, is never without its other half, the right brace, or closing brace. It is typically the case that the left brace is some lines away from its companion right brace. These braces are used to designate what amounts to paragraphs in the C++ language. Left and right braces will be used to enclose special lists.
"…"	The double quote (the quote that is made from two apostrophes). These also come in pairs and typically will enclose some other characters. The ellipsis (…) represents what these characters enclose. Typically, the pair of double quotes enclose a sequence of characters. When you enclose characters in quotes the characters are taken literally – that is to say they are not transformed in any way by the compiler. Never forget to include the closing double quote at the end of the sequence of characters. These also come in pairs and typically will enclose some other characters. The ellipsis (…) represents what the quotes enclose. Typically, the pair of double quotes enclose a sequence of characters. When you enclose characters in quotes the characters are taken literally – that is to say they are not transformed in any way by the compiler. Never forget to include the closing double quote at the end of the sequence of characters. If you do forget the closing quote this will lead to a

<table>
<tr><td></td><td>disaster because the remaining characters that make up your program will be rendered meaningles. The program excerpt show below demonstrates how a compiler will deal with a missing quotation mark.
<pre>Randys-MacBook-Air:~ rkaplan$ g++ HelloWorld.cpp
HelloWorld.cpp:6:11: warning: missing terminating '"' character
      [-Winvalid-pp-token]
  cout << "Hello World\n;
          ^
HelloWorld.cpp:6:11: error: expected expression
1 warning and 1 error generated.</pre></td></tr>
<tr><td>[ ]
(Left and right bracket)</td><td>The left and right bracket is used to identify something called an index. The left and right bracket are always in pairs. The opening bracket must have a closing bracket. Note that the left and right brackets and the left and right braces cannot be used interchangeably. They have different meanings and are used in different places in the sentences you will be writing.</td></tr>
<tr><td>( )
(Left and right parenthesis)</td><td>The left and right parenthesis are used to enclose parts of an expression (as in algebraic expression). The left and right parenthesis are always paired. A left parenthesis is never used without its other half, the right parenthesis. Leaving out a left or right parenthesis of a pair will cause an error in your program. Left and right parenthesis are also used to enclose lists as you will see.</td></tr>
<tr><td>NOTE:</td><td>When you are writing programs it is ALWAYS a good idea when writing paired punctuation symbols like the left and right parenthesis to write both characters of the pair of symbols. This can be a bit tricky as you may not know what you are going to place inside the pair of symbols. The point is that by beginning with the pair of symbols, you will never forget one of the pair. To take care of the problem of not knowing what may go into the symbols, simply leave some space between them when you write them so you have room for what will be written in them.

Examples:
(<br>)
[
]
{</td></tr>
</table>

	}
'c' '\"'	The single apostrophe also always comes in pairs to denote the beginning of a special sequence and the end of a special sequence. This single apostrophe pair typically contains a single character except when the character is an "escaped" character in which case the pair can contain two characters, the first of which is a backslash, and the second of which is a character. When, for example, wanting to display a quotation mark as a quotation character, it must be preceded by a backslash character, followed by the character, followed by the closing single apostrophe.
:	The colon is used as a special purpose punctuation character. It appears in certain sentences to separate certain words from one another. Its use is specific to its purpose therefore we will be describing the colon in the context in which it is used.

Basic Data Types

int
float
double
char
string
void

Vocabulary of C++ Sentences

1. if
2. else
3. for
4. do
5. while
6. switch
7. case
8. cout
9. cin
10. return

Appendix B
Sentences and Paragraphs

A. Declarations
B. Assignment Sentences
C. Conditional Sentences
D. Iteration Sentences
E. Input/Output Sentences
F. Function Declaration Sentence
G. Function Paragraph

Final Examination

Final Examination - Thinking C++ Part I

As I indicated at the beginning of this book there were several reasons that motivated me to write it. One of these was that I believe that a person who professes a belief or practice should follow that practice. So, in my case, one of the practices that I profess is that when you learn something new it should be broken into small enough pieces that so that the pieces are more readily understood - the idea is that the challenge should not be in the learning of the concept per se, but in the understanding of the concept. The more "broken down" the concept is, the better the chance is for the person to learn the concept.

The following examination is to evaluate how well you learned the concepts in this book. We have been trained to treat the word examination as worrisome. I would suggest that it is not a worrisome work but a learning opportunity. Taking the examination is optional but if you do take it, I will be happy to grade it for you. Remember, no computers are to be used – you are to use that wonderful computer we call the "mind" to answer all of the questions and complete all of the exercises.

1. Vocabulary

a. Give an example of the use of a declaration sentence for a single integer variable. You may name the variable whatever you wish.
b. Give an example of the use of a declaration sentence for two integer variables. They should both be declared in the same sentence.
c. Why is it that we call the parts of a C language program sentences?
d. Given an example of the use of the declaration sentence to declare and initialize two variables named abbott and costello as real numbers (double) initializing abbott to 3.2 and costello to 2.7.
e. Of the data types used for variables which data type would you use for variables that will store single characters.
f. What does a variable declaration do? What is its purpose.
g. If you do not declare a variable you use in a program, what will happen?
h. The punctuation used in a declaration with multiple variables is the ____________________.
i. It is possible to declare to variables with the same name (true or false).
j. The word always used to start a conditional sentence is __________________.
k. Iteration is another work for ____________________.

l. The word that is used to cause something to be displayed on the screen is the word ________________.
m. (True or False) Once a variable is declared and initializes, its value can no longer be changed.
n. A variable associates a name with ________________________.
o. The word to accept input from the keyboard is __________.
p. The word to assign a variable to an expression is ___________.
q. An expression is any sequence of characters that can be _____________.
r. Besides the word that begins an input sentence, the symbols that follow the input word are __________.
s. Besides the word that begins an output sentence, the symbols that follow the output word are _________

2. Sentences

Write a C++ sentence to:

a. Check to see if a variable x is negative.

b. Check to see if a variable x is positive.

c. Check to see if a character variable is not a capitalized alphabetic character.

d. Check to see that a variable called score is less than 21.

e. Write down the sentences to score a player's score in a bowling match.

f. A person on the Earth will weight 1/6 of their Earth weight on the moon. Write the expression that will compute a moon weight for a person weighing 200 pounds on Earth.

g. A person buys 3.25 pounds of bananas. Bananas cost .145 per pound. Write an expression that will calculate the total price of the bananas.

h. A board is required that is 6'3/4" in length. You have 4 boards. One of these is 1'1/8", a second board 3', a third board is 6", and a 4th board is 2'15/16". Write an expression that will select the necessary boards that will come close to the total board length needed but not exceed that length.

i. Write an if-sentence that determines if a current configuration of chess pieces is a checkmate configuration.

Paragraphs and Programs

a. Supposing you wanted to have a checkbook on your computer. You would need a program that would allow you to set an initial balance, add to that balance by making a deposit, and subtract from that balance by writing a check or making a withdrawal.

   Write a check book program that allows the following information to be recorded about a transaction.

   1) Date of transaction
   2) Type of transaction (CHK, DEP, WID, CR)
   3) Check #
   4) Paid to
   5) Amount
   6) Running total

   Each of these should be kept in their own array. The main loop of the program is a transaction loop that needs as input a transaction code.

   D – for deposit
   W – for withdrawal
   C – for check
   R – for credit
   E – to erase a transaction

   The program should read in a code (as above) and perform the necessary work to carry out the transaction.

   Remember you are not writing this program to run on a computer.

b. Supposing you were to write a function that compares the values contained in three variables, a, b, and c. The purpose of this function was to compare a to b, b to c, and a to c and return the least of the three values stored in the variables. Also suppose you returned the variable name in which the smallest value was found.

   Now you are to write a second function that returns the smallest value of two arguments, a and b, along with the variable name of the smallest value.

   Finally, the last function returns the variable name of the smallest value.

   You could have something like

   a c b

   where a is the smallest value, c is the second smallest value and b is the largest of the three values. Write a function that returns the sequence of variable names in value order.

c. A maze can be represented by a 2-dimensional array consisting of 1's and 0's. A 1 in a position represents a wall while a 0 in a position represents an open space.

   Part 1. Write a program that will randomly fill an array with 1's and 0's

   Part 2. Write a program that will determine if there is a path through the array beginning at some cell and ending at some other cell.

CPSIA information can be obtained
at www.ICGtesting.com
Printed in the USA
BVOW04s0031050917
493957BV00021BA/406/P